The Financial Services
SHOCKWAVE

Survival Tactics
for Wall Street
and Main Street

JOHN M. WATTS, CLU

PRENTICE-HALL, INC.
Englewood Cliffs, New Jersey 07632

Library of Congress Cataloging-in-Publication Data

Watts, John M. (date)
   The financial services shockwave.

   1. Financial institutions—United States.
2. Finance—United States. I. Title.
HG181.W34 1987   332.1′0973   86–22510
ISBN 0–13–316852–2

Editorial/production supervision and
   interior design: Diana Drew
Cover design: Lundgren Graphics, Ltd.
Manufacturing buyer: Carol Bystrom

The publisher offers discounts on this book when ordered
in bulk quantities. For more information, write:

Special Sales/College Marketing
Prentice-Hall, Inc.
College Technical and Reference Division
Englewood Cliffs, NJ 07632

Printed in the United States of America

10 9 8 7 6 5 4 3 2 1

ISBN 0-13-316852-2   025

Prentice-Hall International (UK) Limited, *London*
Prentice-Hall of Australia Pty. Limited, *Sydney*
Prentice-Hall Canada Inc., *Toronto*
Prentice-Hall Hispanoamericana, S.A., *Mexico*
Prentice-Hall of India Private Limited, *New Delhi*
Prentice-Hall of Japan, Inc., *Tokyo*
Prentice-Hall of Southeast Asia Pte. Ltd., *Singapore*
Editora Prentice-Hall do Brasil, Ltda., *Rio de Janeiro*

Contents

FOREWORD   vii

1 1990: AN ENTIRELY NEW BALL GAME   1

The Crescendo, 3
I Know the Feeling, 3
The Confluence of Change, 4
Behind the Scenes, 11
The Fallout, 12
The World of the 1990's, 14

2 SUPPLIERS: FIVE DOMINANT SURVIVING CATEGORIES   17

The Shakeout, 19
The Bloodbath, 19
The Survivors, 22
For Sure, 32

3 **DELIVERY SYSTEMS: LEAN, MEAN,**
   AND ORGANIZED   **33**

Pain and Agony,   *35*
The Struggle,   *36*
Lean, Mean, and Organized,   *38*

4 **PROFESSIONAL CLUSTERS:**
   A POWERFUL EMERGING FORCE   **57**

Mom and Pop,   *59*
Before Its Time,   *60*
The Evolution,   *62*
The Mother of Invention,   *64*
The Partnership,   *66*
Financial Coordinators,   *66*
A Matter of Efficiency,   *68*
A Matter of Volume,   *69*

5 **THE NEW ORDER:**
   HOW IT WILL FUNCTION   **71**

Run Out of Town,   *73*
Fragile Fabric,   *75*
Fanning the Flames,   *76*
The Gauntlet,   *78*
A Narrowing Field,   *78*
The New Order: How It Will Function,   *80*
You Can Bank On It,   *84*
An Anachronism?,   *86*
Trial and Error,   *88*
Discovery,   *90*
The Rest of the Story,   *93*
A Tsunami,   *97*

6 THE "SLEEPER" THAT WILL REVOLUTIONIZE OUR LIVES 99

Running Free,   101
Kiss the Baby,   102
The Baby Boomers,   102
The State of the Art,   103
The $450 Million Bet,   105
The Snowball,   106
A Walk Into the Future,   107
Here Today,   111
An Era of Freedom,   114
A Time for Reflection,   115

7 A MATTER OF SURVIVAL: THREATS AND OPPORTUNITIES 117

An Uneven Balance,   119
The New Consumer,   120
A Buyer's Market, 125
Boardroom Hysteria,   129
Captives: Dinosaur or Dynamic?,   134
A Declaration of Interdependence,   137
Threats—and More Threats,   144
Opportunities: Few But Golden,   147
Advance Implementation,   148

8 BATTLE PLANS: STRATEGIES AND TACTICS 151

A Mile in Another's Moccasins,   153
Battle Plans,   154
Turning Points,   156
Defensive Tactics,   159
Target Your Present Market,   160
Strengthen Present Relationships,   161

Stay Informed,   166

Strive for Efficiency,   167

Be Technically Competent,   168

Keep Your Train on the Present Track,   168

Offensive Tactics,   169

Innovation,   170

Results: The Only Reliable Yardstick,   171

Analyze Your Present Clientele,   173

Unplug the Decision-Making Process,   174

Pursue Electronic Marketing,   175

Identify Prime Product and Service Suppliers,   176

Fee-Based Practices,   178

Networks: Your Safety Net?,   178

Track the Boomers,   180

Today,   180

Foreword

Those who occasionally review corporate history as a way of predicting the future find it difficult to understand why the movie industry should have fought the new television medium. It is so clear now that motion picture executives should have considered themselves the entertainment industry and welcomed the new medium.

Obviously, they could have swallowed television then and now be earning the millions that have gone instead to the newer television companies.

The same holds true, of course, for railroads and airlines. A little more flexibility, a clearer picture of what might happen in the future, and the railroad companies could have become the giants of a new transportation industry.

We're all familiar with those two examples; some of us say that banking, securities, and insurance executives during the 1970s were also guilty of similar thinking. Financial planning was already becoming a force but the leaders in these three industries at that time disparaged what the pioneers were doing. None assumed the dominant position that was there for the taking.

This is not what John Watts writes about in this book, however. Instead he gives us an insightful and fascinating look, not at the past, but the future of the financial services industry.

Reading his manuscript, I couldn't help thinking how the movie and railroad executives could have benefited if they had had a book such as this written about their future. Executives in the financial services industry today are more farsighted than their predecessors were in the sixties and seventies. I predict that they will not only read this book carefully, but also understand and benefit from what the author is saying.

A book like this doesn't come out very often. The executives smart enough to have John's foresight too seldom combine enough inside knowledge of an industry with the writing ability to produce such a book.

Obviously, it will serve as a guide for top executives and thought leaders in the banking, securities, and insurance segments of the financial services industry. It is my feeling however, that financial planners, stockbrokers, insurance agents, bankers, accountants, and others on the firing line, dealing with the public, will also find a great deal in this book to guide them in their long-range career planning.

Both groups owe a debt to the author for taking the time and sharing so much wisdom and foresight. So much in fact that many in the financial services industry might just avoid mistakes they might otherwise make.

The smart ones will.

LOREN DUNTON
President,
National Center for Financial Education

This is not necessarily as I'd like the
future to be. Rather, it is how I think
it will be, whether I like it or not.
There will be notable exceptions, of course,
to every prediction made in this book.
After the financial services revolution,
we will all know what those exceptions are.
For now, however, we must try to prepare
for the future by anticipating its major
trends. How else can we debate the issues
in advance and be ready for tomorrow?

In that spirit, let's dare to try to look
ahead.

The Author

After the event, even a fool is wise.

Homer

1

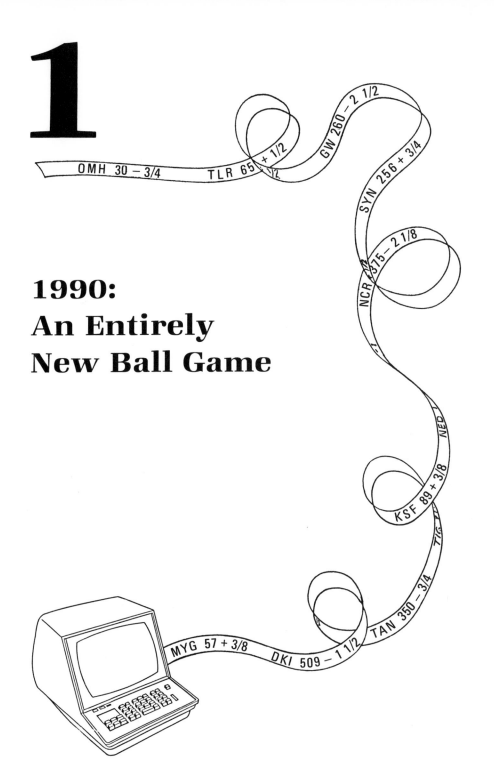

1990:
An Entirely
New Ball Game

OMH 30 − 3/4   TLR 65 + 1/2   GW 260 − 2 1/2   SYN 256 + 3/4   NCR 375 − 2 1/8   NED   KSF 89 + 3/8   TIG   TAN 350 − 3/4   DKI 509 − 1 1/2   MYG 57 + 3/8

• THE CRESCENDO

A random combination of fast moving events is about to come crashing together in the financial services industry. Like a series of unrelated tidal waves speeding toward a common focal point, most of the gigantic forces remain totally submerged and hidden. They will meet soon. When they do, it will cause a crescendo which will thrust companies and distribution systems unexpectedly into a state of chaos, leaving them struggling to find a safe harbor where they can survive and maintain their market share. Unless they understand the invisible forces and act now, small independent distributors of financial services and products—such as those financial planners and insurance agents who operate as sole practitioners—may be the first to drown.

• I KNOW THE FEELING

Although some forecasting is involved, what I'm about to relate is not theory. I'm right in the middle of it and have the scars to prove it. I've learned the hard way about the enormous advantages of being ahead of the tides of change. In the life insurance industry, for example, a product concept known as universal life was invented and published in some detail several years before it revolutionized the marketplace. It remained obscure and ignored until a small but determined group of innovators of which I was a part, brought it to market through some rather untraditional channels in the late 1970s. I remember the discouraging setbacks and rejections we suffered initially but, in retrospect, it was exhilarating to be on the leading edge of massive change. The ensuing battles were waged, fought, won and lost within the following three years. Those many companies and producers who then scoffed were left behind and still today are struggling to regain their previous market share. Others with foresight and the ability to adapt rapidly to change prospered. Independent producers of all types of financial products are now approaching similar crossroads. The time frame to adapt, however, may be shorter. How they prepare and react now will shape their destiny.

• THE CONFLUENCE OF CHANGE

Six diverse, largely unrelated forces are at work to alter your lifestyle forever. All of these changes have been discussed in business magazines, trade journals, professional seminars, and major universities. What has been underestimated is the impact of their simultaneous interaction on the shape of the financial services industry.

• Technology

Electronic linkage, communications, storage and transactional capability: It's all developing at a speed that's mind-boggling. Have you ever heard of "talk-writers"? They are machines that listen to a human voice and instantaneously transcribe that dictation into a final, written text. They are already working in the laboratory and soon will be on the market.

Does the phrase "MSX computer" mean anything to you? The Japanese high-tech industry has "linking" as a key objective in the U.S. market. They plan to combine their MSX microcomputers with laser compact disk television sets so that human personality and emotion may replace the present cold, impersonal form of computer communication. At a cost, I might add, affordable to most homeowners.

If by now your creative juices aren't flowing, stack on these additional facts. There are nearly 20 million microcomputers in homes and offices today, with no sign of the explosion slowing. At least 10 percent of them have telephone modems that connect them through telephone lines to "on-line data bases." They can access up to 3,000 separate databases with dozens of new networks being added every month. Giants like AT&T, Dow Jones, Lockheed, and even the SEC are scrambling both to gain a larger share of the database market and to tie it all together into networks that link computers.

So how does all this affect you? Listen carefully, for here is your first clue to survival. All have the objective of aiming these elaborate networks at marketing—electronic selling, if you prefer. Dow Jones soon will offer discount brokerage services. H&R Block, through its CompuServe subsidiary, already provides electronic shopping, as does Source Telecomputing, owned by Reader's Digest. Millions are being invested and new outlets are being added daily.

The new technology is spreading rapidly, but silently. Like a field mouse escaping the wrath of winter in the comfort of your kitchen, the new technology is already beginning to nibble at your loaf of bread.

• The Economy

Even I would not be fool enough to make a market forecast in a book. I'll let the economists and soothsayers get in trouble all by themselves. Let's assume for a moment, however, that we can rely on two premises. First, the economy and the markets will fluctuate. Second, history (and in particular recent history) may tend to repeat itself. Safe enough?

The financial services industry quite obviously has a direct link to the economy. Consumers adapt their buying, saving and investing patterns in tune with the basic economic cycles. Financial services product suppliers, likewise, have to adjust their marketing tactics to the mood of the consumer. Additionally, the underlying assets of those financial products must be managed in line with the fluctuations of the stock, bond, real estate and virtually all other significant markets.

From the mid-1940s through the late 1960s, financial services management was a piece of cake. Relatively prosperous times, healthy markets, low inflation, and rising consumer incomes combined to make it a fairly simple task. With a few exceptions, the financial services industry became lazy and unimaginative. Why not? If one can prosper with no more effort than burning up time in committee meetings and building elaborate bureaucracies, why take the risk of aggressive management? It was a grand era, with banks and insurance companies erecting magnificent home office edifices while stockbrokerages portrayed the image of mussing their pinstripes only by clipping coupons.

Then change entered the scene, catching most off guard. Inflation became a more serious factor and the markets became more volatile. The velocity and frequency of economic cycles gradually increased. The first victims were the stockbrokerage firms, unable to cope with higher costs and a loss of the status quo. Mergers reduced many long-established NYSE firms to a single phrase within the long, alphabet-like names of the successor companies.

Change is a traumatic thing. None of us relish it, particularly when it is thrust upon us unexpectedly. The early 1970s gave me my first taste of a lesson I hope I never forget. I ask you to learn from it too, because your

open-mindedness and flexibility will hold your key to survival during the coming financial services revolution. I was Director of Marketing of a large mutual fund complex that had enjoyed growth and profit during the mutual fund popularity of the previous two decades. Our registered representatives were "stockjockeys" of the first order, having lived their professional lives in a period of steadily rising stock markets. Then came what many still refer to as the "crash of '69." Stock mutual fund prices plummeted. The public wouldn't touch them with a ten foot pole. Knowing no other product to sell, our field force was starving.

In desperation I turned my attention to another market: bonds. We had a small and inactive, but relatively well performing bond mutual fund in the family. We noticed that closed-end bond funds were selling like hot cakes, so we felt a bond mutual fund might also. I called in the regional vice presidents and presented my idea. They rejected it totally. It was an insult, they protested, to ask an equity-oriented registered representative to sell anything as mundane as a bond fund. They returned to the comfort of their regional offices and sales continued to decline.

As you will discover within the coming few years, there arrives a time when one must either "bite the bullet" or shrink into obscurity. I decided to bypass the RVP's and sell the idea directly to the field force. I changed the dividend payment to monthly, the P.R. department came up with the slogan "More Money More Often," we divided the home office troops into road-show teams and introduced the new campaign nationwide. With the tradition-bound RVP's still protesting the invasion of their territories, $100 million in sales exploded from the effort. The RVP's could not change what years of tradition had riveted into their brains. The markets had changed but the RVP's couldn't. Most, now, are in other lines of work.

The economic shocks of the last fifteen years have every possibility of repeating themselves in the future, adding to the chaos which is about to emerge throughout

the financial services business. Just ask any banking or insurance executive, for example, if life will ever be the same after the disintermediation of 1980. The billions of dollars which swelled the coffers of money market funds were pulled suddenly from their portfolios, leaving many thrifts, banks, and insurance companies on the verge of insolvency.

Things change. They will continue to do so on the economic front, probably with greater frequency.

• Deregulation

In general, I'm for deregulation. Not everyone enjoys it, however. Just ask Braniff, Continental, or the other airlines who needed protection under Chapter 11 when that industry went through it. Like it or not, you will experience the same sort of situation when the individual components of the financial services industry see the legislative and regulatory barriers that have always separated and protected them come tumbling down. Most segments and special interest trade groups are still fighting, but to little avail. Those regulations and separations which make sense will remain. The others will disappear. It is inevitable.

During the rapid realignment that followed the airline deregulation, new carriers sprang up almost overnight while established firms were faced with daily critical decisions which would alter their futures forever. Continental, for example, came out of voluntary bankruptcy a stronger entity, while Eastern (which never utilized Chapter 11) found the competitive new environment almost overwhelming.

When the flood gates open in our industry, you had better not be standing in the way of the torrent. Fierce competition will erupt and the law of the jungle will prevail. The courageous, cunning, and strong will become dominant while the weak are devoured totally. The entire financial services industry will be restructured.

Will there be a place for you in the strange, new

world? Don't worry. That's what this book is all about. Only the unwary and the unprepared will be trapped. Unfortunately, they will be many. Foresight: That's the key word for the achievers of tomorrow. Join them. Tomorrow is becoming quite visible for those who will let their logic and ingenuity run.

• Legislation

It used to be so nice—so comfortable. Congress would pass a new tax law, we would have months to absorb it, and any ambiguities would be solved by the Treasury Department in a year—or two—or three. Even our past improprieties were "grandfathered." Then we could settle down once again to several years of relative stability.

No more. The government is desperate for new revenues. Consumer groups are exposing real and imagined abuses. Sacred cows are being sliced methodically and tossed to the wolves. The frequency of new legislation is increasing to the point that there is a surprise around every corner.

This state of affairs will continue into the 1990s. Virtually every segment of the financial services industry will find itself continuously under the microscope of those who see an opportunity to squeeze out another tax dollar or two.

The consumers—your clients—will watch this cauldron with great interest. They will become more aware and more wary.

• Demographics

Want to talk about change? Look at what's happening to our population. Add a little technology to the picture and you'll see it change even faster. There will be large numbers of employees, for example, working out of their homes hundreds, and perhaps even thousands, of miles from their traditional place of employment. Present-day social patterns involving neighbors, family, and fellow employees will be broken. No longer will people be tied to geographical centers, making it impossible to physically contact many of those within your present group of clients. More on that later.

Today the so-called baby boomers are the group to watch. They make up one third of the U.S. population and by 1990 their ages will range from the late twenties to the mid forties. Together they will comprise America's most powerful group in terms of purchasing power. They will be more wealthy and better informed than their counterparts of the past. Personal, face-to-face service will be less important to them in their busy lives, so they will develop a price sensitive attitude toward financial products. They will demand efficiency, quality, and fairness. They will be tough customers.

Yes, things are changing. The old norms and methods soon will be gone forever. It may be hard for some of us to adjust, but we'd better get used to the new order: Independent-thinking consumers; a high proportion of dual career households; smaller families, yet more homes headed by a single adult; fewer geographical restrictions; direct, impersonal marketing; dependence on technology. The good old days are gone with the wind.

- **Consumer Knowledge,
  Attitudes, and Habits**

Already the buying habits of the baby boomers are starting to change the character of the financial services business. Recent surveys indicate that baby boomers are beginning to become receptive to distribution methods that do not involve face-to-face contact. Three in ten of them, in fact, have purchased financial services and products offered through the mail or via telemarketing. That ratio is expected to increase rapidly.

They are not alone. Their independent, free-thinking attitudes are beginning to spread throughout the population. Middle income America, for example, now accounts for over one half of all household purchases of financial services and products. And who is trying to wrap their arms tightly around this group? The so-called financial services centers, such as those of Sears—even Penney and K-Mart. The banks are not far behind.

The consumer of 1990 will be tied less to old norms and loyalties. Price and convenience will be paramount. The fact that 12 percent of today's teenagers now own a home computer should be screaming out to you that the household of the 1990s will be equipped and comfortable with new forms of communication. With access to countless databases from their own homes, tomorrow's consumers will be better informed and able to stay up to date continuously.

Luckily for you, most consumers don't yet realize all of this. One day soon they will wake up with a start and see the power they hold. They are moving rapidly toward that moment. Don't let them leave you behind.

- **BEHIND THE SCENES**

It's like an iceberg silently, but relentlessly, drifting toward its destined encounter with a hapless ocean liner. The top strategists in all segments of the financial services industry are planning, plotting, and positioning behind the scenes. The majority of corporate "insider" time, in fact, is presently being devoted to constructing major pieces of the new order. Few talk publicly about it. The $400 billion in net revenues generated annually by the financial services industry is at stake. Huge investments are being placed on the gaming table. It is the calm before the storm.

Not that a few preliminary skirmishes don't break out occasionally to give us a clue that war is about to be declared. The former chief executive officer of one of America's largest banks is reported to have said:

> . . . the insurance lobby reacts with a lemming instinct in order to protect its antiquated distribution

network and to stifle competition, all to the consumer's disadvantage. . . . I recently told the insurance industry itself that you can limit the public's convenience only as long as they know of no alternative. Once the public knows and realizes that all that's standing between them and convenience is some government regulation, either the regulation will change or the government will.

Does anyone out there think for a moment that the banks are not deadly serious about expanding their influence throughout the entire financial services marketplace? They are not alone. There are other major players just as determined. It threatens to be a bloody battlefield. There will be many casualties.

Fortunately, the major trends are becoming visible. Certain forces are clearly dominant, giving us enough advance warning to fortify our positions and build our defenses. Only then can we develop our battle plans.

First, let's take a glimpse at the fallout. After the smoke clears, the survivors will wake up in a new financial services world dominated by these characteristics. Once they are understood we will then be in the position to draw a complete picture of our industry as it will be structured and as it will operate in the 1990s and beyond.

• THE FALLOUT

Earlier, we explored together the six largely unrelated forces shaping the future and we took a glimpse at the intense positioning taking place within the inner sanctums of the corporate headquarters of financial services companies. The combination of these diverse forces and the current strategic planning will produce the following dominant industry characteristics:

• An absolute dependence on modern technology for survival.

- Huge capitalization needs to develop and support that technology.
- Totally new methods of conducting business.
- New players entering the game, causing intense competition.
- Mergers and consolidations for survival.
- Pressures to lower distribution costs (including commissions) drastically.
- A focus on productivity: ways to move more volume through fewer distributors.
- Price-conscious consumers viewing products as commodities.

It's not as futuristic as it first appears. Already these new industry characteristics are falling into place. While many of us are still eyeing the automatic teller machines with distrust, for example, 60,000 of our fellow Americans are using their personal computers to handle virtually all of their banking transactions, almost automatically, from the comfort and convenience of their homes. Such giants as Bank of America, Citibank, Chase Manhattan, and many others are expanding their services and competing for customers.

Need to pay bills? Certainly, you don't plan to waste time by addressing envelopes and licking stamps. Just turn on your personal computer, type in the payee's code name, add a dollar amount, press an execution key and presto!—the bill is paid instantly—anytime, workdays or weekends, 24 hours a day. If need be, bills can be paid from thousands of miles away. Never again will your account drop below a minimum balance by mistake or will you be embarrassed by an accidental overdraft. Your computer sees to all that. Having trouble keeping accurate, accessible records? No longer must it be a problem. When the bill is paid, the bank's program can automatically categorize it for easy recall or for plugging into the appropriate space on your income tax return.

New technology is arriving upon the scene at a pace too rapid for any of us to completely absorb.

Mergers and consolidations may be more pronounced in the future, but they are already occurring in record numbers. New financial services companies are already popping up on every corner. Unencumbered by old ways, unprofitable inventories, and huge home office structures, these new players are introducing us to new slants and methods for conducting our business. In some cases, they are also introducing new risks. The pressures for lower cost and more efficient ways of doing business are already highly visible.

In the chaos and confusion which will develop as these forces become more pronounced, a few traditional, service-oriented pockets of the old way may continue to exist. These, however, will be special situations that fit a specific need or market. People will continue to be willing to pay extra for a service not available elsewhere and tailored to their special desires. Even in these rare instances, however, there will be a demand for automation, efficiency, and productivity never before required of—or even imagined by—the financial services business. The consumer is becoming more knowledgeable of the many facets of our industry. They will be smarter, more shrewd, and, particularly when it comes to price and value, more demanding.

Open your eyes. It's happening now. Get used to it, it's going to get worse. Prepare yourself.

• **THE WORLD OF THE 1990'S**

Massive, almost overpowering new distribution systems will emerge, driven by huge conglomerates, bank holding companies, and producer cooperatives. Certain markets will become dominated totally by specialized, sophisticated organizations with marketing techniques targeted at particular occupational, geographic, and income groups. No one in the financial services industry will be able to remain totally independent. Survival will be the greatest challenge for most independent producers and financial planners, but unprecedented opportunity awaits those few who can visualize the future and prepare now.

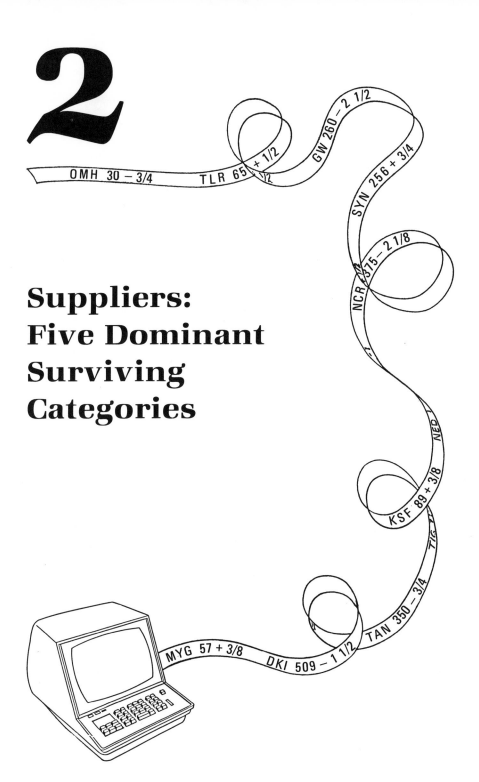

2

Suppliers:
Five Dominant
Surviving
Categories

• THE SHAKEOUT

Those who thought the financial services shakeout of 1980 was traumatic "ain't seen nothin' yet." The current desperate struggle to reduce home office overhead and distribution costs is in direct conflict with the need for massive capital investments in data processing and modern technological equipment. The situation will come to a head soon, resulting in mergers, acquisitions, informal networking, and, in some cases, outright liquidation. Add to that the new competitive forces that are joining the fray and you are about to witness total chaos.

• THE BLOODBATH

It has already started, actually. A prestigious financial publication, for example, recently described the trauma in one segment of the financial services industry as ". . . the most prolonged insurance industry bloodbath within memory." Referring to the property/casualty business, they described ". . . six years of almost insane competition. . ." and reported that ". . . horrified investors sold off huge blocks of p/c holdings." It's all cyclical, of course, but the cycles in all segments of financial services are getting longer and suffering deeper troughs.

As just another current example, bank failures, until recently, were unheard of. Now banks and thrifts are folding in record numbers, with the remnants being bailed out by the government or merged into larger institutions. Do you think it is over? The folly of billions of dollars of unsecured loans to shaky foreign governments hasn't even come home to roost yet.

Look around and you will see many other examples. The symptoms include high traditional overhead costs in the face of increasing competition and lower profit margins on products. Another is the difficulty of managing the assets backing the issuance of financial instruments to the public during times of volatile interest rates and intense economic cycles. The easy days are far behind us, having fled with the decade of the 1970s. The days of the "riskless" investment are over, yet many have failed to learn from the bitter experiences of their professional peers.

Soothsaying is a hazardous exercise, but I will risk laying one prediction on you. Some insurance companies still are issuing billions of dollars worth of instruments known as single premium deferred annuities. The typical certificate or policy guarantees the principal (cash value) at book value, less a small surrender charge. To be able to offer competitive interest rates, a few of those insurance companies then invest the assets in long maturity bonds. What happens if a year or two later interest rates go through the ceiling? Several things occur simultaneously.

First, the market value of the underlying bonds owned by the insurance companies drops into the cellar. Most people don't understand that a corporate bond guarantees an interest rate and the return of the invested principal at maturity date, but does not guarantee the principal value in the interval between the purchase date and the maturity date. The market decides that value and it fluctuates widely based on the difference between the bond interest rate and the currently prevailing market interest rates on new money being invested. The longer the time to the bond's maturity date, the more volatile are the fluctuations. If current interest rates go up, the principal value of bonds issued earlier at lower rates drops, and vice versa. So what happens to those insurance companies if interest rates rise significantly? The companies become locked into the lower yields on the bonds, cannot afford to sell them at deep discounts, and, therefore, cannot raise the customers' yields to currently competitive levels.

Now look at it from the customers' point of view. They are not locked in. Had current interest rates declined, they would have held on tightly to their present annuities to enjoy the higher rates. But instead, rates rose. In such a scenario, the insurance companies now have guaranteed a cash value far in excess of the current market value of the bonds. After subtracting the small surrender charge even semi-sophisticated policyowners realize that they can cash in those annuities and reinvest the proceeds elsewhere at much higher current interest rates. That is exactly what they could do—suddenly—like a run on the bank.

And who would take a multi-million dollar hit to their surplus? Those few foolish insurance companies which felt they could outguess the market and now must sell those deep discount bonds to pay the higher, book valued guarantees. A company which issued a billion dollars worth of single premium annuities and subsequently invested the money imprudently could easily see itself faced suddenly with a $300 million loss. Some do not have deep enough pockets to make it. I fervently hope that I am wrong and that it will not happen. But at least in a few isolated instances, it will.

It is only fair to add that the vast majority of insurance companies which offer both annual premium and single premium annuities do so safely and prudently. That portion of their business does not dominate their balance sheet and the assets are invested so as to match income and maturities to contract liabilities. Unfortunately, however, it is often the exceptions that make the headlines.

One thing is for sure. The next few years will be fascinating to watch if you are not at the wrong place at the wrong time.

• THE SURVIVORS

When the dust settles there will be fewer, but generally larger, companies manufacturing financial products. All whose fortunes depend upon the distribution of these products had better understand the implications. The surviving companies will play the multiple roles of being your competition, your sources for all products, and the providers of most financial services. The mold has been poured and the outlines of the pattern are becoming visible. By analyzing their operating patterns and distribution methods, I have been able to group the suppliers of the future into five distinct categories. Get to know them. Some will be your allies. Others will attempt to bury you.

Wholesalers

This category actually is nothing new. By 1990, however, it will become much more crowded than it is now. Many companies have depended upon a national field force made up of full-time career salespeople to distribute their products. The costs of recruiting, training, managing, housing, and maintaining high levels of commissions, however, have become prohibitive for many of the smaller financial services companies. Those companies which either are unable or unwilling to try to raise the productivity of the average salesperson are already taking steps to abandon this type of distribution system.

The Wholesalers are characterized by the absence of a captive sales force. They either never had or no longer will have a fully controlled distribution system. The companies in this category, therefore, will find their niche by attempting to be the very best in a relatively narrow field. They will manufacture either one or a small family of related financial products, such as real estate limited partnerships, a family of mutual funds, or a specialized insurance portfolio. Neither owning nor controlling any distribution system, they will depend upon supplying their product through others' outlets, franchising agreements, networks and independent agents.

The ranks of the Wholesaler category are swelling because the industry buzz words these days are "alternate distribution systems." Translated into English, that means there are hundreds of companies simultaneously searching for new, less expensive outlets for their products. It has been a rather interesting scramble to watch, particularly for independent distributors and the many small financial services shops which have been set up by salespeople who formerly were "captives" of a single company.

I have watched the life insurance industry go through this exercise and I am fascinated. After spending tons of money on research and spending hours locked in strategy sessions, the majority seem to have come up with the identical "alternate distribution system." They have decided to take a hard run at the small, independent, personally producing general agent. After all, it does seem to make financial sense. The companies don't have to house them, train them, or pay them a salary. Just romance them with good products, high commissions, and complete services, and the production comes flowing in. At first blush, it seems ideal. In actuality, it is not working out that way.

With so many companies going after a limited number of producers, competition is entering the scene. The romancing is getting expensive. As enticements, the life insurance companies are offering general agents juicy commission contracts, zingy products, and sophisticated support packages such as computer hardware backed up by elaborate proposal systems. The attractiveness of these enticements is drawing new agents into the independent ranks, but not in great enough numbers to offset the appetites of so many insurance companies going after a single distribution outlet.

The independents, of course, are loving this extraordinary attention. They are thriving on it and prospering. If you think about it a bit, the ultimate end result is rather obvious. The personally producing general agent is going to get whipsawed.

The whole objective of going after this alternate distribution system was to lower the cost of distribution. Instead, the multi-company competition is driving costs up, not down. A few life companies who have adopted this strategy are back in the conference rooms scratching their heads over the problem. Most, however, are going full steam ahead, losing money on certain product lines but hoping to "make it up in volume." In this scenario, the light at the end of the tunnel definitely is another train. The inevitable head-on collision will leave many independent agents high and dry as companies either withdraw from this market or slash commissions and withdraw support packages. Some companies may hesitate too long, finding themselves in the thick of the financial services revolution without a viable, cost-efficient method of distributing their products.

The companies which remain within the Wholesaler category after the shakeout will distribute their products in one or more of several ways. Surviving independent agents, obviously, will be one outlet. Most property and casualty insurance companies already distribute in this manner and the surviving companies will continue to do so in the future. They will be joined by many other types of manufacturers of financial products and services. Their strategy, however, will be to move more product at much less cost through fewer producers.

Another popular distribution method of the Wholesalers will be providing products for sale through the distribution systems of other companies. This already is the prime distribution method for many mutual funds and limited partnership tax shelters. Entire corporate complexes have been created, for example, just to provide those specialized product lines to NYSE member firms. The suppliers manufacture and the stockbrokerages distribute. It is seemingly a perfect marriage but, as the suppliers do not control the distributors, it can often be a tenuous relationship. It will continue to work well for some, however, and other suppliers will attempt to play this game.

The diversified financial services complexes, described under the Generalists category below, will be among the types of suppliers that do maintain a full-time, captive, career sales force. They will attempt to manufacture and distribute the full spectrum of financial products and services. Even the Generalists, however, cannot efficiently manufacture every type of specialized financial instrument. For very specialized lines, therefore, they will turn to smaller, boutique manufacturers (another type of Wholesaler) that provide one unique product to many such distribution systems.

Another profitable slot that many product manufacturers will find in the future will be in the role of phantom suppliers. Under this arrangement the Wholesaler, generally a specialist in a unique product line, will package the product under the label of the distributing company. The phantom supplier provides the product, the entire administrative support system and even the customer service—all in the name of the clients' financial services company. This relieves the large distributor of the burden of manufacturing a minor, but perhaps important, specialized product. Simultaneously, for the phantom supplier, the distribution clout and the prestigious name of the larger distributor produce high volume at a reasonable distribution cost.

Discounters

Watch out, financial services world. Here come the Discounters. Already the no-load mutual funds account for almost 75 percent of all mutual fund assets. Discount stockbrokers didn't even exist in 1975, yet today their market share of retail trading volume is exploding. As just one example of the "future shock" of rapid change, the SEC recently predicted that discount brokers would capture over 20 percent of the $6 billion in securities trading by 1990. In actuality, they have over 25 percent now! By 1990 they probably will have captured over 50 percent of the market.

No product area remains untouched. Life insurance is being mass-merchandised through employers to the extent that today over one third of the total number of life insurance policies sold are through employers. No-load tax shelters are already being distributed through some banks and no-load life insurance is available from fee-based financial planning practices.

It is just the beginning. Discounters will be a major force in the marketplace of the 1990s. Comprising a diverse group of companies, this category is distinguished by its focus on various forms of mass merchandising. Some will provide a broad array of financial products to a very targeted audience, such as USAA does with military personnel. Others will distribute specialized product lines on a no-load basis via advertising, direct mail, telemarketing, and electronic marketing. Many more companies which manufacture financial products will join the Discounters in an attempt to find low-cost methods of distribution.

As the consumer becomes more wary, informed, and price conscious, more discounted and mass-merchandised products and services will become available. See the picture starting to develop?

The diversity of types of Discounters can range as far as your mind can expand. There will be specialty types of Discounters which go after one specific market. They will target that market, whether it be occupational, social, or geographical, and provide a narrow band of products aimed specifically at that audience. Others will aim their marketing thrust via advertising on a national basis. While most such systems have no third party intermediary (they bypass the salesperson entirely), others such as payroll deduction product suppliers will use mass enrollers. Virtually every identifiable group or association through which a list of names may be assembled will be a prime target for Discounters.

Present-day, established Discounters are expanding their product lines. T. Rowe Price, an established no-load mutual fund sponsor, recently joined Sears in offering a no-load real estate income fund. Many other companies which historically have used salespeople in their distribution efforts are now secretly doing feasibility studies on their potential in the Discounter environment. Outside influences are adding to the momentum. The Florida Supreme Court not long ago struck down a state law that prohibited insurance agents from rebating all or a portion of their commissions to customers. Certain consumer groups are determined to extend the concept to other states. Expect soon, therefore, to see a new form of marketing entity known as an insurance discount brokerage house. The pressure continues to mount for price, and price alone, to be king in the financial services marketplace.

Merchandisers

Characterized by a tendency to merchandise totally unrelated products side by side through a single distribution outlet, the Merchandisers as a group threaten to capture and dominate the huge "middle American" financial services market.

Sears confidently has announced that it expects the financial services centers located in their Sears stores to be a major factor in making it one of the nation's very largest financial services firms. After successfully conducting a test market with such centers in eight of its stores, Sears has now expanded the number significantly. Each of its financial services centers is staffed by representatives of Dean Witter, Allstate, and Coldwell Banker. Stocks, insurance, real estate, and a myriad of other financial products are all in one place, backed up by a trained staff to help you make your buying decisions on the spot. Young couples with dual careers often do their shopping together, so the financial services set-up is very convenient for them. It is also attractive to women in general. They enjoy browsing and they have a high comfort level with a name such as Sears. As they also control the majority of wealth in this country, is there any doubt in your mind that the Sears financial services concept will be successful? Soon it will be copied by virtually every other type of merchandiser in the country. It's a sickening thought, but I wouldn't be surprised one day to be able to purchase financial services while traveling with my car through the local car wash.

It would require major legislative changes for them to reach this point, but those banks and thrift institutions who hope to manufacture a diverse line of financial products in the future would also fit into the Merchandisers category. I get such a kick out of the current activities of most of the banks attempting to expand their horizons. Like many embryonic marketing programs, it is strictly a trial and error situation—false starts and retreats. I have had the opportunity to hear the presentations of several major banks and thrifts in regard to their plans to enter the insurance and securities markets. So grandiose are many of the schemes, and so rudimentary are the suggested strategies, that at times the proposals have been almost laughable. The flow of naive ideas seems endless.

Does this mean that you do not have to worry about the banks as future competitors? Absolutely not! You had better be scared to death. They are going to be right in the middle of all your markets and they're going to be there in force. They are determined and their commitments are well financed. Right now the banking industry is exerting most of its energies in trying to change the laws and regulations which currently prevent it from going full force into the financial services business. There is fierce infighting and lobbying going on behind the scenes. Some informed observers are convinced the banks will be successful. If they are, they will be one of the most formidable product suppliers in the financial services industry.

In the meantime, the banks and thrifts are doing what I refer to as "tire kicking" in the financial services markets. They are allowing certain insurance and investment companies to set up shop in their lobbies to sell financial products to their customers. The banks' piece of the action usually is rent, but that payment is often geared to the amount of business that the suppliers actually conduct through their lobbies. Other banking organizations are starting to furnish their customer lists for similar activities via direct mail. There must be a thousand schemes going on at this point.

What most of us don't realize at this time is that the banks and thrifts simply are toying with us right now. They're letting us come in to help them learn. They will watch us make our mistakes, see us break the ice and then—when the regulatory climate is right—they will dump us like a sack of potatoes. Thump! Boy, will there be some red faces in the insurance industry when those who have made huge commitments to that form of distribution find out that they were just being used as temporary teachers and trailblazers. All that time, energy, and money invested, but once the banks learn enough— thump! They're dumped.

The big banks and thrifts have every intention of being manufacturers of financial products and services in their own right. Denied that, they still intend to remain in the business as distributors. In addition, they fully intend to make these financial inventories available to the smaller banks and thrifts through their correspondent systems. The whole network already is set up for them. All they need is the knowledge and the experience.

Banks, department stores, and maybe even car washes: Soon they will be adding enormous new competitive pressures to the financial services marketplace.

Chapter 2

Generalists

The Generalists will be the totally self-contained financial services complexes. Their objective will be to provide a total array of financial merchandise and planning services while simultaneously owning and controlling their own distribution systems. The Generalists will epitomize the manufacturing and supplying of total financial services and products primarily intended for the upscale market.

American Express is one of the formidable contenders in this category. They have acquired Shearson, a prestigious NYSE member firm; Firemen's Fund, one of the nation's largest property and casualty insurers; and IDS, a Minneapolis based mutual fund and insurance firm. Each of these major companies within their conglomerate has its own established field force and each targets its efforts toward a distinct marketplace. Add that complex to the millions of American Express cardholders and it doesn't take much imagination to see American Express cutting a wide swath through the marketplace. Eventually they will get their act together, and, when they do the financial services world will feel the tremors.

As mentioned earlier, many insurance companies have decided that they can no longer afford the cost and relatively low productivity of their captive career sales forces. Others, however, feel that they can keep theirs intact by enhancing productivity and adding totally new financial services and products to their portfolios. All insurance companies which do plan to maintain a career sales force, in fact, will be forced to become Generalists. Productivity is the key. If their sales people can learn to sell more types of products to each client in their files, those insurance companies will be able to afford and maintain that type of distribution outlet. Productivity . . . productivity . . . productivity. Those firms and producers who get the message soon enough will prosper.

Stockbrokerage houses underscore that message. Although many major firms engage in lines of business such as investment banking which do not require a retail sales force, most still rely heavily on stockbrokers smiling and dialing at the branch level. Frequent reminders in the form of red ink on the bottom line have gotten the message to the wire houses that the individual productivity of the average broker is vital. Merrill Lynch, for example, has announced that they will expect each broker to generate $250,000 in commissions annually to justify holding a position with Merrill as a stockbroker. Those firms which also learn the lesson that their massive home office bureaucracies must be curtailed will be the survivors and will join the ranks of the Generalists. Those who do not wake up may end up being owned by bank or insurance holding companies.

Although a few Generalists will target other markets, most will aim at the higher income consumer. If that's where your efforts are directed be prepared to contend with them. They will attempt to dominate the affluent market.

Vendors

An entirely new subculture is developing from within the financial services industry, and it will grow to be a major force by 1990. The Vendors will be the firms who provide a broad range of services, yet manufacture no products.

The more obvious of the Vendors of today are the software firms who develop and supply the many computer programs which keep the wheels of the financial services industry rolling. Financial services consulting firms are also increasing in number as the complexity of our industry intensifies. These consulting firms will flourish, at least for a short while during the revolution, when certain financial services companies finally realize they are in trouble and scream for help.

The Vendors of the future include the suppliers of the many data bases which will instantaneously provide research and current market data to virtually every office and most households. Future suppliers of the necessary equipment and transmission lines for electronic marketing fall into this category.

Some surprise entrants to the scene will include CPA partnerships, law firms, and other professional groups who plan to develop the capability of providing full financial counseling. They will distribute no products, but their appeal will be the offering of unbiased financial advice to their clients. Once again, the target market will be upscale, adding more chaos to the already boiling financial pot. These firms fully intend to take fee-based financial planning directly to their customers—and to yours.

The Vendors: Many will support you; some will compete with you. A few will send continuous data directly to your customers so that your clients may measure your performance.

• FOR SURE

Only a few things are "for sure" in the crystal ball for financial services suppliers: massive change, chaos, and trauma. Some companies will emerge as complete losers. Others will be lucky to survive, and a few will have won big. New players are popping up behind every bush. A cost crunch, fewer support services, and a commission squeeze are all on the horizon.

Don't slam the book shut yet. There is hope and opportunity for you.

3

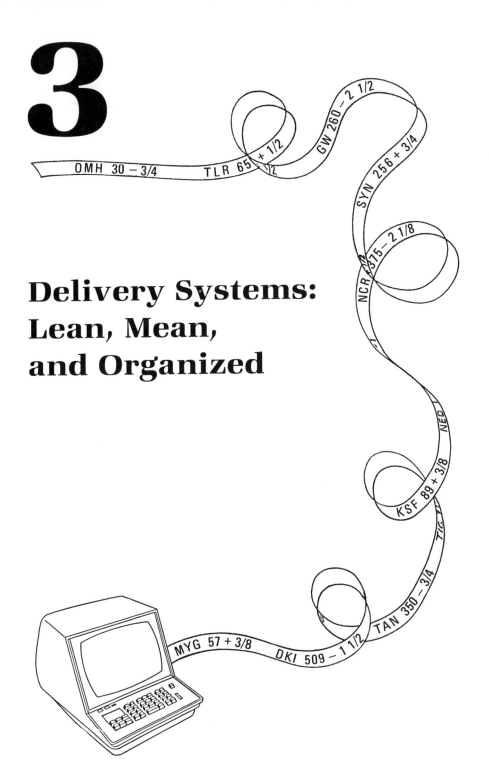

OMH 30 – 3/4   TLR 65 + 1/2   GW 260 – 2 1/2   SYN 256 + 3/4   NCR 375 – 2 1/8   NED 1   KSF 89 + 3/8   TIG   TAN 350 – 3/4   DKI 509 – 1 1/2   MYG 57 + 3/8

Delivery Systems:
Lean, Mean,
and Organized

• PAIN AND AGONY

The scope of the massive changes already taking place and about to be implemented in delivery methods is vastly underestimated. Discussed very little outside the inner sanctums of corporate headquarters, these changes are just beginning to be felt at some distribution levels. Let's face it: No one likes to talk about pain and agony, but I'll share some with you. It's only fair; you'll feel it before long.

One of my more recent challenges involved a turn-around effort for a major insurance company. A household name organization, they were old, successful, very structured, and characteristically traditional. Suddenly their world had changed. Traditional methods and inflation, combined with a consumer demand for lower margin products, caused profit margins to shrink rapidly. My assignment? Simple enough. Just lower overhead by a few million dollars while multiplying sales results. By concentrating on productivity rather than tradition, and utilizing available technology, we did it. Premiums doubled, productivity rose, and costs declined. The company will survive and grow in the future, providing careers for professionals and quality products for consumers. That's the good news.

So where is the pain and agony in this happy story? In massive, rapid change. Those who were flexible, well informed and natural high achievers prospered. Those who were tied to the old ways, either through lethargy or stubbornness, were left behind. Jobs were lost and career ambitions, futile as they may have been, were dashed. Failing to heed the many advance warnings, these people were caught by surprise. They were not intellectually or psychologically ready for radically new ways of doing things.

Don't let it happen to you. That type of example will be repeated and multiplied a thousandfold between now and the early 1990s. Delivery systems of today will so change as to be barely recognizable a few years from now. From huge conglomerates to individual producers, everyone will be affected. Some will perish while others will prosper.

• THE STRUGGLE

At this point it is almost like a clandestine revolutionary tactic, with virtually all major financial institutions desperately trying to prepare for the battle which is certain to come. Most recognize that there must be a new order of things very soon. The old ways are far too inefficient and expensive. The cyclical, fickle economy holds a new surprise around every corner. Simultaneously, a new breed of sophisticated consumer is prepared to wreak disintermediation havoc upon those naive institutions still clinging to the old ways. As they demand lower-margined financial products, those consumers will watch, with little remorse, the death of those lethargic, overly structured companies too steeped in years of inefficient tradition to change.

A massive, yet silent, struggle has begun. Research teams and high-level strategic planning groups lay out the new road map, while line management strives to keep the existing distribution systems running profitably. Thousands of pilot programs are being launched cautiously in an effort to discover the way of the future.

For decades Metropolitan Life had distributed its products exclusively through its own captive full-time career sales force. In early 1985, however, the management announced through advertisements in trade journals that for the first time they were going to market their complete line of life insurance products through independent agents and brokers throughout the United States. Although they didn't announce it in their advertisements, what they obviously were trying to do was to add a less expensive alternate distribution system to their existing marketing methods. It probably was a gut wrenching decision for Metropolitan. Breaking many years of tradition is not easy. With this announcement, of course, one more company—this time a giant—joined in the race to capture the attention of the growing number of independent life insurance producers. The financial services industry has tended over the years to follow the herd instinct. The majority have come to the decision that they must go after the independent producer in an attempt to lower distribution costs. By all doing so simultaneously, however, they may very well alter the supply and demand curve.

In the desperate search for less expensive ways to distribute products, some innovative pilot programs do surface. Many of them center around the many kinds of deals that are being cut between banks and insurance companies. Recently, a modernistic new program was announced with the objective of mass-merchandising insurance products through a shared ATM (automatic teller machine) network. The shared network is owned jointly by three banks and there are reportedly over one million names in the network. Initially, the banks plan to distribute such insurance products as homeowners, auto, medical, and accidental death policies through this innovative marketing outlet. The basic assumption is that the market is becoming consumer-driven and is greatly influenced by price. With this direct method of distribution (leaving out the salesperson), those packaged products will be delivered to the consumer at premiums generally below the market average. The banks predict a response rate of between three and six percent, with a conversion rate on those responses of up to 30 percent. If they are right, it will be a very successful program. The banks will be particularly delighted, because they will make money on the pilot program and the insurance industry will have educated and trained them. Then, if bank deregulation progresses far enough, they will toss out those insurance companies (hopefully, at least, with a "thank you") and continue the program themselves.

Not all of the pilot programs have been successful. That is the purpose of innovating and piloting, of course. You learn by experience. Those successful programs will be expanded, and even the failures help the newcomers in the market to find their ultimate niche. Some of them, however, are finding the learning experience rather expensive. Two major banks in the northeast recently learned the hard way of the pitfalls of plunging into non-traditional banking areas. Both had decided to move forcefully into the mutual fund marketplace and, after the fact, found that processing the accounts was no piece of cake. Dividends that should have been paid sometimes weren't. The banks couldn't keep up with the daily accounting involved every time someone bought or sold shares. Finally regulators intervened, and when the dust settled one bank had suffered a $2 million hit against earnings. The other bank eventually lost $1.3 million. No one ever said it would be easy. Such is the cost of the financial services revolution.

• LEAN, MEAN, AND ORGANIZED

"Delivery systems." That includes you, doesn't it? Be ready. Step with me into the immediate future and let's visualize the seven types of predominant distribution methods which will be operating then. Two are so new, so significant, and so formidable that each has a subsequent chapter devoted to it.

All seven of the delivery systems of the future have only three things in common, but it is these elements that will allow them to survive into the 1990s: All are lean, mean, and organized. They will be lean: They will trim distribution costs and run with an efficiency never seen before in the financial services industry. Unprecedented competition will guarantee this. The resulting commission squeeze will force delivery systems (whether they be large groups or small independents) to operate with equal or greater efficiency.

Tomorrow's distribution systems will be mean. They will be highly competitive and ever aggressive. It will be a matter of survival of the fittest. Every delivery system and even every individual producer will strive to be on the leading edge of the marketplace. Constant change will become the norm. Innovation and flexibility will be the keystones to success.

Successful distribution systems will also be highly organized. The day of the truly independent producer who operates in a vacuum apart from all other influences will be gone forever. The successful survivors into 1990 will have to have a relationship with some group, cooperative, or association which provides group bargaining power, management information, and electronic access to product information and support systems.

Actually, the shape of the delivery systems of the future is becoming quite clear. Those of us behind the scenes who have been silently preparing have compared notes enough to envision where the entire marketplace is going and where literally millions of dollars will be committed. Make no mistake about it. The following seven categories will be the only types of distribution methods which will survive into the 1990s. All others will be abandoned.

First we must understand. Later we can draw up the battle plans.

Captives

"Captives" is a rather unfair term because in our free enterprise system, and particularly within the current turbulent financial services industry, no salesperson is ever held in bondage. It is the recognized industry term, however, for those full-time career distribution systems which voluntarily distribute the products of just one manufacturer directly to the consumer. Included are most stockbrokers, many life insurance agents, some property and casualty agents, a few major mutual fund houses, and most of the real estate industry.

Let's start with the life insurance industry. Is the so-called agency system dead? As we presently know it, yes. Let me explain. As we presently know it, the traditional career agency system lacks two of the three essential ingredients mentioned above. It is not very "mean" and it is far from being "lean." Efficiency, responsiveness, and innovation must replace the lethargic bureaucratic structures which have characterized their home offices. In the field, productivity must replace greed. Demands for the host companies to simultaneously provide the highest commissions, the most competitive of products, and cradle-to-grave security must cease. Field-generated marketing ingenuity and a burning desire to solve client problems must become paramount.

Productivity and efficiency: I cannot repeat that phrase often enough or overstress its importance. Yet home offices continue to strangle from obesity and entire career field forces seem bent on a blind, suicidal tendency to demand silver slippers with which to tiptoe gingerly and gently through the financial services revolution. As a result, many insurance companies which have relied upon full-time career, exclusive sales forces have started abandoning them. In the future such captive distribution systems will belong only to those complexes which are able to form a partnership between themselves (the host suppliers) and their distribution systems. Loyalty, mutual trust, and a fierce determination to succeed: Combine those attributes with our "productivity and efficiency" phrase to arrive at the secret formula for those Generalists of the future who will maintain a captive field force.

The life insurance industry is not the only financial services segment that has depended on career sales distribution systems, but it is the largest. In the 1990s fewer insurance companies will depend on that method to distribute their products, and most who do will have still other alternate distribution methods to help strengthen their balance sheets. The agency system of the future, of course, will be greatly altered from its traditional configuration. A massive consolidation of agencies has already begun. Most major life insurance companies have experienced a 40 percent reduction in the number of manpower agencies during the last decade, and within the next five years the further reductions could be as great as 70 percent. This trend indicates that a company that had 300 separate agencies in the mid-1970s will have reduced that number to approximately fifty by 1990. The survivors, of course, will be much larger in size than the present-day agencies and they will be managed by highly trained professional executives. As each agency will be covering a much larger geographical territory, there will be detached groups of producers scattered throughout the territory who are linked via computer to the large mega-agency. It will be a well-oiled machine.

The life insurance industry, of course, will not be alone in undergoing this consolidation and drastic reduction of such captive sales forces. Recently the Securities Industry Association commissioned a study of what forces would shape the industry's future. The conclusion? Much the same as was outlined for the life insurance industry above. Productivity and efficiency will be the rule of the day. Furthermore, the study indicates that the larger securities firms will tend to dominate a much larger market share of the sales revenue than they do today. It recognizes that competition will be the major driving force for change in the securities industry and that "diversified financial services companies" will be the fiercest competitors.

Which brings me to my point. Only a relatively few stockbrokerages and insurance companies will maintain full-time career, exclusive sales forces. That luxury will primarily belong to the giants, but they will be joined by a few determined smaller companies who have joined in partnership with their Captives to solve the productivity problem. Those giants of the future will be the financial services conglomerates. The smaller company contingent will both manufacture primary product lines and broker a wider spectrum of products for distribution. Whether they were known formerly as an insurance company, a stockbrokerage house or a family of companies, in the future they will be able to afford a full-time sales force only if they are a full financial services provider, i.e., a Generalist. The product and distribution differences which separated them in the past will disappear. All will have to offer full product lines and services.

This is what these firms will look like in the early 1990s. Sales office centers will be large, highly automated, and supervised by a staff of skilled professionals. Only those salespeople who maintain an unprecedented high level of productivity will survive. There will be time for very little one-on-one selling unless the customer is willing to come by the sales office. Much like stockbrokers operate today, most transactions and customer contact will be taken care of over the telephone. Each salesperson will be required to handle a full product line, possibly also offering professional services for a fee. Each will be supported by sophisticated computer programs which make available both sales and technical information to assist in closing sales and servicing clients.

Highly productive salespeople will be able to survive and prosper in such an environment. Some think that Merrill Lynch is being unreasonable by requiring that each salesperson produce $250,000 in gross commissions. By the early 1990s, that figure could be much greater for each captive salesperson who plans to work for any financial services complex. The Generalists will be tough taskmasters, but the real winners may be the well-paid Captives of tomorrow.

Yes, the so-called Captive salesperson of today will be gone. Those who survive into the future will be working for a smaller number of financial services firms which will require them to sell a full spectrum of products and maintain a productivity level unheard of today. The results? Most of the Captives of tomorrow will find a market niche that can be exploited with efficiency. Many will aim for the upper income markets. They will capture a major share of it.

Financial Centers

"Buy your stocks where you buy your socks." That won't be a joke for long because it's already starting to work. The consumer is responding. This will be one of the major delivery systems of the future. When fully operative, this type of convenient outlet will intensify competition greatly.

Sears is the most visible pioneer in this unique method of delivering financial products to the consumer. Commenting on the financial services industry, D. F. Craib, Chairman of Allstate, recently said: "We're in an awkward period of transition." Mr. Craib must be a master of understatement. We are in the middle of a revolution which is about to jump from behind the bushes and break into open warfare. It is a fight for the consumers' dollars and Sears is one of the innovators leading the charge. It is worth exploring some of the other comments Mr. Craib made because he makes a lot of sense. He observed that one of Sears' goals in creating their financial centers was to stress convenience in their contacts with their customers. In his words:

That means meeting clients on their own turf, where and when they want to do business. The sociological changes of the past twenty years, the increase in two-income families, single-parent families, and the hectic pace of life in general, mean that we're finally going to have to conform to our customer's schedule, instead of expecting to do business the other way around.

In short, Sears is after the huge baby-boomer market. In my opinion, they and others who follow this concept will make a major dent in it. In Mr. Craib's own words: "The winners will be those who appreciate—and act on—the customer's desire for greater choice and more convenience, a less intimidating and/or forthright approach to investing, and a lasting relationship built on commitment and trust."

Do not for a moment think that Sears is alone. You've heard, of course, that a similar technique is being tried by Penney, Kroger, and K-Mart. You have also heard that several insurance companies are setting up arrangements with banks whereby agents can cool their heels in bank lobbies, hoping that some of the customers will buy insurance. Much more, however, is going on that you may not have heard about. Let me give you just one example.

Not long ago, through a strange set of circumstances, I had the privilege of being invited by the president of a large bank to visit what he called a "model branch" which he felt was the forerunner of the future. "Now keep it quiet," he implored, "because I don't want the insurance agents in this part of the country getting all upset. I'd rather that right now they didn't know what I was doing." I promised to protect his anonymity and not even to divulge the section of the country involved. The concept, however, is fascinating. Soon you may see it bursting out all over America.

It was magnificent. Located in its own building which blended with and was located on the fringes of a middle-class residential neighborhood, it was exquisitely furnished. On closer examination, however, it contained a cleverly balanced mixture of the comforts of the old bank lobby and the modernistic technological features of the future. Outside were three drive-in stations, two equipped with ATM's, but one staffed by the traditional teller smiling through the glass panels. One more ATM was located near the front door. As we entered the lobby, the teller counters were immediately ahead. Tastefully displayed in lighted signs above their heads, however, was something I'd never seen before. The string of signs offered a whole potpourri of financial services: discount brokerage, insurance, mortgages, CD's, mutual funds, and prime checking accounts.

Immediately, I looked around for the insurance desk which might be prominently displaying a sign which said "Lloyd's of Lubbock" or "Rigor Mortis Mutual." There was none. Instead, as I looked to my left, there were the normal bank officers' desks and behind those the typical vault containing the safe-deposit boxes. As I looked to my right, however, a vision of the future came more clearly into view. There, in the center of the aisle which led to the offices, was a large cabinet (much like a cooking island located in the middle of some kitchens, yet much larger) which contained additional displays along with some CRT's and several keyboards. On one side of the island you could pick up the telephone, punch a button which corresponded with a number on a display and get a full recorded explanation of the service or product being offered. Walking around to the other side, I found a stock quote machine available for the use of customers along with current stock market information. Oh, yes, there was a telephone there for placing trade orders. It was comfortable. It was convenient. It was very well done.

Wait just a moment. Who did the selling? Where was the insurance desk in the lobby? I must admit that there were properly licensed (rather, I should say, multiple-licensed) financial counselors located in the offices behind the electronic island console. What was unique about this system, however, was that this model branch had concentrated on cross-training every person in that branch (including the tellers) in every product and service being offered. No, they were not experts. But they did understand the products in general and they were trained to recognize a client need when one was mentioned. They were service oriented, but they never failed to ask if the customer might have a need for one of the other products.

In short, every individual in that bank was trained to be a salesperson. When a specialized need was identified, the customer was introduced to one of the more knowledgeable financial counselors who resided in the offices behind the console. So hush-hush, yet already in full operation!

The financial service centers threaten to capture the vast majority of the financial dollars of the huge middle-income market. And who exactly comprises that market? By 1990 it will be the baby boomers who have come of age to dominate that market. Convenience and price are their primary desires. Already middle-income America accounts for more than half of all household financial purchases. By 1990 it will be a much greater percentage. The financial service centers will be after it all.

Do you think you might have problems in the coming fiercely competitive market? Read on.

Direct Response

Price and convenience. Those two words keep raising their ugly heads and by 1990 you will hear them being screamed from the rooftops. Consumer attitudes and preferences are changing rapidly. Price: Assuming a volume of sales can be maintained, what better way is there to trim the price than by eliminating the salesperson from the formula? Convenience: What could be more convenient than having the supplier go directly to the consumer? It allows shopping through the mails or purchasing needed financial products via payroll deduction at the place of employment. The possibilities of market coverage and product availability range as far as our imagination can run.

One major no-load mutual fund organization recently made an attempt to sell no-load life insurance through the mail. The American Association of Retired Persons successfully markets a myriad of financial products in large volume directly to its millions of members. A large regional bank sold tax-deferred annuities through the mail to its customers. Earlier in this book we discussed the amazing inroads being made by discount brokers and explored the pilot program through which life insurance companies will join the banks to directly market insurance products through a shared ATM network.

This is just the beginning. The search for more efficient distribution methods is driving more and more companies toward a direct form of distribution which eliminates sales representatives entirely.

Mass merchandising is included in this category and takes many forms, ranging from direct mail through telemarketing and payroll savings. The movement will spread like a prairie fire in the next few years. It will be driven by the winds of pressure on companies to lower distribution costs and operate more efficiently. It will be kindled, of course, by an increasingly fickle, price conscious consumer. Virtually all financial services institutions will be involved, either as a primary line or hidden in the activities of a subsidiary. Up to now it has been the almost exclusive territory of no-load mutual funds, but they are being joined by banks, S&L's, credit unions, life insurance companies, tax-shelter distributors, property and casualty insurance underwriters, and many more.

And what is their hope, dream and deep-seated ambition? To eliminate you entirely. They are rapidly making inroads.

Videotex

Recently I attended a high-level executive meeting of a major financial services association to participate in a discussion of five-year strategic planning. When the subject of future distribution systems came up, I recommended that some research and development time be devoted to the subjects of Videotex and teletext. The response? It was unanimous: Blank stares and an awkward silence. The older, more traditional generation of executives simply cannot visualize it. It is here and they cannot see it. It may inundate them, yet they cannot grapple with it. They are in for the surprise of their lives. Come to think of it, you may be too!

These initial stages of the financial services revolution move so silently, yet so swiftly. Almost unnoticed, the smart money has been bet on Videotex. Although it was made public on Valentine's Day, 1984, it revealed much more than just a casual love affair. These people mean business—big business. On that day, IBM, Sears, and CBS joined together in a project to develop a nationwide Videotex service for households which are equipped with personal computers. Targeted to begin in 1986, it will be a major step forward for the infant Videotex business, which is now expected to explode into a $30 billion industry by the early 1990s.

"Videotex" is computer assisted electronic marketing—and so much more—sent directly to the convenience of one's home or office. You have heard so little about it, yet it will alter your lifestyle forever. Professionally, it confronts you with both a dire, perhaps lethal, threat and, simultaneously, for those prepared, an opportunity to find the highway to your dreams.

More—much more—on Videotex later.

Indirect

As mentioned above, the cost of maintaining a full-time career sales force is becoming prohibitive for all but the most efficient financial services firms. The vast majority of companies, therefore, have been scrambling desperately to open up alternate distribution channels. As explored earlier, most have selected the route of going after independent general agents and financial planners. Others have made major commitments to direct response as a delivery system. Still others are carving out their place in the future via a distribution method which I refer to as Indirect. Indirect involves several techniques, ranging from using others' sales forces to working through intermediary marketing groups.

With the birth of many smaller, specialized financial

services companies, independent marketing groups have sprung up which act as the intermediary between the supplier and the actual retailer in carrying the product to market. They are specialized distribution companies who have gained access to various distribution systems and can deliver to those systems the products from several different financial product suppliers. They can move product in volume for a smaller markup than would be needed for individual sales people.

A few years ago, some former associates of mine formed such a company to merchandise various products through NYSE member firms. First they made contact with several different major insurance companies to come up with a specialized line of products that would be slightly unique to their group. In return for some financing from these companies, they made certain commitments in sales volume. Then they hired young salespeople throughout the country to work only on an override basis within an assigned geographical territory. Once this system was in place, they called on the headquarters of target stockbrokerage firms to make their distribution arrangements. Their appeal was twofold. First of all, they would bring quality products to the stockbrokerage firms. Second, their representatives throughout the country would call on the various branch offices of those member firms to get the individual stockbrokers trained and motivated. It made sense to the insurance carriers involved because the override they paid the intermediary group was much less than the cost of carrying a full-time distribution system. For the stockbrokerage firms, it provided the necessary training resources to move more products through their stockbrokers. With so many products available, the NYSE member firms must rely on outside training assistance for product education and training. To them, it is a less expensive alternative than trying to staff a huge training department with experts in all of their many products.

Phantom arrangements also are becoming popular as an Indirect method of distribution. As mentioned in the last chapter, this has become a distribution method for many specialized companies that cannot afford a captive distribution system. Through these phantom supplier arrangements a manufacturer of products develops a "private label" for another firm which does have a large distribution system. As specialists, they can develop, underwrite, and administer the product more cheaply than the larger firm could. The larger firm benefits by the lower product development cost and the smaller, specialized firm finds a market for its products through the label and distribution outlet of another company.

More and more financial institutions are opting to become only manufacturers and are seeking to find other distribution outlets for their products. One major life insurance company, for example, purchased a minority interest in certain NYSE member firms in order to obtain access to those distribution systems. Again, it was a two-way street. For the stockbrokerage firms, the insurance company provided protection against an unfriendly acquisition from outside. In return, the insurance company received exclusive marketing agreements for the distribution of its products.

Indirect delivery systems: You will see more of them in years to come.

Independents

Yes, Virginia, there still will be Independents. Not as you and I know them, however, for there will be very few truly independent producers.

During the early 1980s economic disruption, a product revolution, and the evolution of financial planning as a profession caused the population of independent producers to multiply rapidly. Their growth and prosperity were spurred by the desperate rush of most insurance companies to find and romance independent producers as alternate distribution systems. Today these many new financial planners, general agents, and smaller broker-dealers are flourishing as product manufacturers heap high commissions, competitive products, full home office support, and computer software systems upon them.

Supply and demand are about to enter the picture. The competition among companies for the attention of these independents is pushing distribution costs up, not down. During the second half of the decade the competitive pressures of new suppliers and innovative delivery systems entering the marketplace will reverse the process suddenly and precipitously. In terms of the numbers of independent producers, there will be an implosion. Their numbers will shrink more rapidly than they grew just a few years before.

Life insurance general agents and independent financial planners still have a little time left, because additional life insurance companies are entering the contest for their attention on almost a daily basis. For property and casualty independent agents, however, it is another story. The devastating earnings crunch of the major P&C companies in recent years has forced those companies to begin the weeding out process even before the life insurance industry realizes that the same thing will have to happen on their side of the fence. In a recent survey conducted by the "Big I" (the P&C Association of Independent Agents), the following trends were noted: The average size of the P&C agency continues to rise rapidly. Simultaneously, there are fewer and fewer small agencies. Terminations of agency contracts by insurance companies are up markedly and it is the "little guy" that is being eliminated. It is just a matter of time before the same trend is started by the life insurance companies.

It is ironic, somehow. So many companies are going after the independent general agent and financial planner, yet the very actions of those same companies are designed ultimately to drive the independent producer to extinction. The independents are being used, almost in desperation, as an interim step until the confused companies discover their ultimate, lower cost method of distribution. The companies' strategic planners know that they must deliver the product more cheaply and in bigger volume. As a result, those producers who are small or weak soon will be ignored completely, though they need the support the most. The majority of independents suddenly will be shocked to find themselves forced out of business. It will happen suddenly and only the strong will survive.

After the dust settles there will be a few truly independent financial planners and insurance agents remaining, but mostly in isolated, rural areas. In towns and cities of any size, their survival as Independents, and even their very existence, will depend on finding some way to join together with others in a common purpose.

The wise and the well prepared will prosper as their peers disappear from the scene. They will have discovered that surviving involves the utilization of available technology and networking techniques.

Networks

I was relaxing in the easy chair in my den about 6:30 p.m. one Tuesday evening, sipping a glass of wine in an attempt to unwind from a hectic day before dinner. The phone rang. "All I need. Probably another business call," I grumbled to myself. When I picked up the phone, I was pleasantly surprised to hear the voice of a friend and former business associate of many years past. It was Charlie, at the time the most successful regional vice president for one of the large, household name life insurance companies.

"I've got to come see you, John," Charlie erupted nervously.

"Why, anytime, Charlie. I'd love to see you and it would be fun to talk about not only old times but what's happened to us both in the ensuing fifteen years. When are you going to be in this area?"

"I've got to see you and I've got to see you fast," Charlie spat out nervously. "How about this Thursday? Can I stay with you folks?"

Obviously I was surprised. I glanced at Jan, she indicated the calendar was clear, and so I said: "Of course, Charlie. Let me know what flight you're coming in on and I'll either pick you up from the airport myself or see that someone is there to meet you."

Thus a nationwide Network was begun. Charlie's company, despite their glorious and successful past, had decided to abandon their traditional life distribution system suddenly and completely. Charlie and all of his associates were soon to be out of a job. Most in his position would have felt defeated and, at least for some time, would have retreated into remorseful seclusion. But not Charlie. He had an idea and he wanted my company to back him up. We did, and in the process picked up, at very low cost, a new national distribution system.

In short, here is what Charlie put together. Bitterness from his recent "reward" for outstanding past achievement brought him rapidly to the conclusion that he never wanted to be an employee of any major corporation again. Instead, he contacted all of the key members of the abandoned distribution system and formed a highly organized networking system. Each of those individuals felt as Charlie did. They wanted to remain independent and they did so. But they had the extra force of the Network. We provided them a specialized product line, and, when a national account situation arose, the Network was recruited to implement the marketing program on a nationwide basis. They had the best of both worlds: their independence as general agents and the networking clout of a major national organization when banding together would provide them that strength.

That's what networking is: an informal banding together of Independents to give them economies of scale, needed technology, national clout, and up-to-date, proprietary information. In the future, Independents other than those in small rural communities will find a networking system mandatory to survival and prosperity. They will have to have the economies of scale to compete with the new lean and mean delivery systems that are about to enter the market. Their group power, however, can give them influence in product development, power in negotiating contracts with suppliers, access to computer systems, and even some national advertising when appropriate. Technology will be a major factor in the financial services business in the future, and as a group the Independents will be able to access the data base networks which will provide transactional and electronic marketing capability. Through the Network they can get access to new customers, tap into management system data bases and even, as a group, afford to conduct due diligence investigations to insure that the products they carry are suitable for their customers.

Networking will take many forms. Its beginnings may be seen in broker-dealer organizations which have been formed to provide buying power and investigative ability for otherwise relatively independent registered representatives. It will grow to encompass an entirely new form of financial planning organization which I call professional clusters.

Professional associations and trade groups, such as those of the financial planning, securities and insurance segments, could be one form of network to aid independent producers. To date, however, such associations have shown little propensity for playing that role. A second form of Network could be informal joint ventures formed between producers in a certain locale to provide the buying power to tap into data bases, software packages and contracts for products. More common will be the producer cooperative, where each member remains independent, but is bound by decisions of the majority of the cooperative. The farmers have worked this way for years. Insurance agents and financial planners will have to learn how to put it together, and they had better start fast because there is very little time left.

Franchises have been growing in popularity in recent years and do constitute a more formal kind of Network. Some independence still is retained, but there is a greater degree of subservience to the franchising group. The advantage, of course, is the ability to operate with the recognition and power of a national organization. And then the new kid on the block will enter the scene soon and add a degree of sophistication never before seen in the financial services industry. It is the professional cluster and the next chapter of this book will be devoted to it.

An interesting anomaly is that so many companies are dismantling their full-time Captive or career type distribution systems at the very time when such homogeneous, interdependent groups can provide marketing strength. Those same companies are opting for, dealing with, and depending upon the independent, sole proprietor producer, who is soon to be an endangered species. Instead, their efforts should be aimed at injecting new standards of efficiency and high levels of productivity into their existing Captive systems. Once made financially viable, the Captive system of distribution is in actuality the most formal and strongest form of Network.

The key will be banding together, either formally or informally, to obtain group buying power, electronic communication and transaction ability, software packages, research, management systems, and much more. For sole practitioners in particular, Networks hold the key to a bright and successful future for those who do not remain in (or return to) a Captive system.

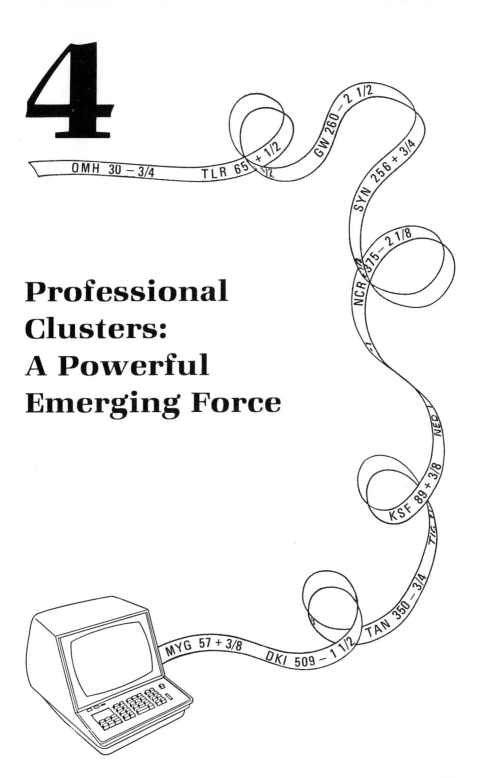

4

Professional Clusters: A Powerful Emerging Force

• MOM AND POP

Today there are tens of thousands of financial services mom and pop operations: independent insurance agencies, financial planners, and small brokerage firms. By the early 1990s there will be very few. They cannot exist with rising costs, lower commissions, and a narrow band of products. It will be a matter of rapid, painful, multiple starvation: Starved by the sheer inefficiency of traditional methods; starved by the loss of market share to Discounters and Generalists; starved by being cut off from the mainstream by technological advances they cannot comprehend or afford; even starved by being abandoned suddenly by the very product suppliers which today are romancing them and showering them with favors.

The marginal producers will have to find employment in entirely new lines of work, and, for the sake of efficiency in the financial services industry, perhaps that is as it should be. Many sales professionals will return to their original homes within Captive systems. Others will be hired as brokerage intermediaries by Wholesale suppliers, employed as enrollers by certain Discounters, or absorbed by one of the premier marketing groups of the future: the professional cluster.

• **BEFORE ITS TIME**

I think it was back in the mid- or late 1960s when an extraordinary venture was launched in the financial services industry. It was a brilliant idea conceived by people of vision. Unfortunately, as it turned out, it apparently was a concept twenty years or so ahead of its time. Although not identical in concept, it may very well prove to have been the forerunner of the professional cluster, a delivery system which will evolve from and constitute the ultimate form of Network.

As I remember it, the company was known as Financial Services Corporation (FSC) and it was founded in Atlanta by some pioneers in the financial planning movement. They had on their staff a representative of virtually all of the professional disciplines that make up a complete financial planning and estate conservation team: CPA's, attorneys, CLU's, and others. The concept was to deal with the upscale, business and professional markets by providing a one-stop, complete financial plan along with implementation recommendations. The salesperson or financial planner in the field would gather complete data from the client, and send it to Atlanta, and a tailored financial plan and action recommendations would be put together by the team of professionals. Revenues for the company reportedly were generated from two sources: fees for the professional services and a commission override on the many products that were sold. FSC was founded, apparently, to serve both as a fee-based financial planning service and as a supplier of the products sold when the financial recommendations were implemented.

I do not remember all of the details, but apparently the world was not quite ready. Both the consumer and the agents were tied to customary ways of doing things and fees for this type of professional service were hard to generate. Furthermore, the field representatives needed to have rather broad financial services knowledge, but we were still in the era of product specialization. On top of all that, the insurance companies and other financial institutions tended to rebel against the concept because it constituted a threat to their traditional (yet very profitable) distribution methods. It was an idea before its time and FSC eventually shrank into obscurity.

Take note, now, of the advantages of being flexible and adaptable to change. As we come closer to the time of the financial services Armageddon, flexibility and forward thinking will be mandatory for the survivors. Yes, FSC survived. It is alive and well today, but not in the same form in which it was conceived. As I understand it, the FSC of today is operating as a combination managing general agent and securities broker-dealer, supplying primarily registered products to NASD licensed representatives. It is interesting to note that most of these registered representatives actually are insurance agents who have had the foresight to know that they must supply more products to their customers than just the traditional insurance portfolio. Many, as I understand it, actually still are full-time agents and general agents of major insurance companies, but they also carry a full portfolio of registered products such as mutual funds and tax shelters. Most of their insurance business goes to their primary company, but excess insurance coverages and all of the registered products are supplied through their relationship with FSC. I wouldn't be surprised if, at some time in the future, FSC gradually reverts to its original concept and becomes a premier fee-based financial planning firm in addition to being a product distributor. Not quite a professional cluster, but close in concept.

• THE EVOLUTION

Together let's walk through the evolution of an informal relationship into the professional cluster of the future. There are many simultaneous forces at work pushing many professionals in this direction. Those who recognize it first and have the organizational skills to put it together will build personal fortunes for themselves.

Bob, John, Sam, and Paul live in a typical American city which embraces a metropolitan area of approximately one and a half million people. They are friends, both socially through their country club connections and professionally by the fact that they share many of the same clients. Bob is a Chartered Life Underwriter who, over the years, has built a comfortable insurance practice for himself as a general agent for a leading insurance company. John is a CPA with an accounting practice which serves both individuals and small businesses. Sam has his own law firm which is a small, but successful, tax practice. Paul formerly was a stockbroker, but during the last five years he has been operating as a small securities dealer which provides his clients NASD type products and private real estate limited partnerships. Although they are each independent financial services professonals, they tend to serve an overlapping, relatively affluent client base and none of the four views any of the others as direct competitors.

Bob, John, Sam, and Paul all belong to the local Estate Planning Council and over the years they have formed the habit of gathering together after each monthly meeting. During their private monthly session, they confer with one another in confidence about the financial planning problems and challenges currently facing them in specific client situations. Together they work out their clients' needs and problems, in the process referring their clients back and forth to one another when that specific area of professional expertise would be helpful to the client. What they have accomplished, on a very informal basis, is a referral system when it is in the interests of the client to obtain the counsel of one of the other specialists. They find it a very comfortable relationship which enhances their own professionalism and is beneficial to the referred clients.

One evening at the Estate Planning Council meeting the guest speaker was the proprietor of a very successful, fee-based financial planning practice. Representing the National Center for Financial Education, the guest spoke of both the growing financial planning profession and the need that the typical American consumer has for a structured, planned method for accumulating assets. After that meeting, in their private session, Sam broached the subject of providing a more complete and structured financial planning package for his clients. He suggested that when a client appeared to have the need for a total program, the four professionals could work together on a more formal basis to produce a complete, written financial analysis and a series of recommendations for that client. It would be a fee-based service with the charge to each customer based on the time each professional spent on preparing that specific package and recommendation.

The idea worked. It worked so well, in fact, that the four found they had to hire a writer and a paralegal to prepare the narrative portions of each formal financial plan. For the first time, they found themselves bound together in a more structured relationship. Each maintained his own independent practice, yet in partnership they ran the small firm which generated the financial plans. They didn't quite realize it yet, but they had just formed a Network.

The next steps in the evolutionary process were rather obvious. Gradually, their jointly held financial planning firm found it necessary to purchase computers and then tie those computers via telephone modems into various data bases to obtain up-to-date market and financial information, as well as to tap into financial planning and estate conservation software packages. As the firm grew, they discovered almost accidentally that by banding together they achieved a certain amount of bargaining power when dealing with Vendors and Wholesalers which provided their services and products. The financial planning practice had become a mature operation which, incidentally, was consuming more and more of their time and professional attention. Gradually, almost imperceptibly, their independent practices shrank and the new firm became the center of their professional lives.

It was smooth sailing for the next two years. Several things then happened at once. First of all, the firm's expanding client base started to demand both more quality in financial recommendations and more value in financial products. At the same time that the overhead costs of the financial planning practice were rising, the clients themselves were becoming much more price conscious. Product suppliers were responding to the same consumer pressures by cutting margins and building in much lower commission allowances. Bob, John, Sam, and Paul were perplexed as they felt financial pressures squeezing the profitability of their financial planning firm. In response, this brain trust of professionals decided to leave town for the weekend to think through their problems, do some open brainstorming and try to come up with a solution.

• THE MOTHER OF INVENTION

It has been said a thousand times over the years and it is so true: Necessity is the mother of invention. In their brainstorming meetings, our four hypothetical professional partners discovered the forces at work which would require them to change their modus operandi. Here are some of the things that they identified.

They had already discovered the need for forming a Network. It gave them economies of scale, efficiency, the joint resources to access vital data base linkages, group bargaining power, and even new markets. In their private meeting they discovered some other obvious problems.

First of all, there seemed to be a proliferation of new financial products hitting the market at a mind-boggling pace. Even these experts, with their diverse backgrounds, found it almost impossible to be an authority on several hundred diverse financial products while simultaneously trying to keep up with the technicalities of their own professions. With the commission and distribution cost squeeze of the products they handled, they also determined that somehow they would have to find a way to move a much higher volume of products at a much lower cost. Actually, this applied to their financial planning professional recommendations as well as to products. Another factor that they identified was the extreme competition that was developing throughout the marketplace. People seemed to be buying products in the strangest places, such as in department stores, banks, electronically through their personal computers, and even through direct mail solicitations. Everybody seemed to be getting into the act.

There seemed to be conflicting demands. With the need for efficiency, there was really no time left to "prospect" for new clients. Even for professional people, the so-called prospecting activity had always consumed far too much time. There had to be a better way. The four men searched for an answer. They needed efficiency, yet they had to serve a relatively affluent market which demanded more attention and tailored service than could be supplied by most individual practitioners, mass-merchandising firms, financial service centers, or even the futuristic forms of electronic marketing.

Finally, the four partners found the answer. As a result of this weekend of secluded brainstorming, they were able to identify the problems and form the initial strategies and tactics for forming a professional cluster. It had the potential to grow into a major, nationwide firm by the early 1990s. Necessity is the mother of invention. The forces at work in the marketplace make the evolution into the professional cluster of the future inevitable.

• THE PARTNERSHIP

No, you won't find it in the financial services dictionary. Professional cluster is a new term. In a way, you can equate it to today's large law partnerships and the "Big 8" accounting firms. Some of those firms, in fact, may themselves start professional cluster organizations as collateral business to their normal professional practices. Additionally, some professional clusters may be sponsored silently by groups of certain Wholesale suppliers. Most, however, will be founded by entrepreneurs who band together with other professionals to tap the combined talents of the entire group while simultaneously increasing the efficiency of product distribution and the utilization of their professional expertise.

At the core of the professional cluster will be a small group of professionals (the partners), each a recognized expert in a specialized professional field such as tax law, accounting, insurance, estate planning, employee benefits, or various types of investments. The partners are responsible for the recommendations made to clients, although they themselves meet only the most select and affluent customers on a personal, face-to-face basis. The vast majority of financial plans and recommendations are prepared by computer, based on data which is fed in from detailed financial questionnaires which pinpoint the resources and objectives of each individual client.

• FINANCIAL COORDINATORS

The small core of partners is backed up in the larger professional clusters by an army of financial coordinators who are responsible for the direct contact work with the vast majority of clients. The financial coordinator contacts the client—most often by phone or even electronic marketing methods, stimulates interest in the need for financial planning, gathers the data on a comprehensive questionnaire, and submits it electronically to the head office mainframe computer. The financial plan and recommendations then are prepared completely by a computer from programs both created internally and tapped through a series of data bases. Any unusual or special needs situations that cannot be solved by the computer network are highlighted and will be reviewed by a specialist at the head office level prior to the time the completed document is returned to the financial coordinator. The complete plan is then reviewed in detail with the client and, for specific product recommendations, the sale is closed. If additional professional assistance is required, such as the preparation of wills or the handling of other legal needs, the client is advised by the financial coordinator to communicate (often electronically) directly with the home office law partner or other staff attorney. Virtually all professional financial services are offered and the full spectrum of financial products is sold. It is the ultimate in achieving, within one organization, the coverage of nearly the entire financial services industry, as well as the services of the legal and accounting professions. Revenues are generated from fees for the preparation of financial plans and the offering of specific professional advice, as well as from commissions generated from the sale of products as the recommendations are implemented.

You may be wondering at this point how these salespeople can be trained to be experts in so many diverse financial and professional fields. The answer is rather obvious: They can't. Rather, they will be trained financial counselors who have only a broad working knowledge of the entire spectrum of the financial services industry, as well as the various professions. They will be trained to recognize a need, reinforce a sense of urgency on the part of the client, and motivate the client to purchase the services of the professional cluster. They will then gather the financial data, enter it into the head office mainframe computer and screening system, receive the printout recommendations, and close the product sale. Financial coordinators will be good at customer relations and have an instinct for identifying financial needs, but they will be trained primarily to be superb closers.

• A MATTER OF EFFICIENCY

In order to grasp the entire concept of the professional cluster, it is important to keep in mind that the financial coordinator does only the customer contact work which results in a sale of a product or service. Everything else will be done by other specialists. Gone forever will be the day when salespeople will be able to afford to spend 75 to 80 percent of their time prospecting for new clients. The efficiencies demanded by tomorrow's financial services world will not allow it.

The high sales and fee volume which will be necessary for the operation of professional clusters will require the utilization of a specialized head office team that does nothing but generate qualified leads. The team will be a group of sales professionals that are trained not only to surface prospects, but also to get them interested to the point of agreeing to have a contact made by a financial coordinator. Direct response techniques will be used, targeting affluent neighborhoods and businesses. Additionally, there will be full-time telemarketers who screen potential clients via the telephone and certain electronic communications methods. For carefully selected high-income groups, seminars will continue to be utilized to create in the minds of potential customers the urgency of a counseling session with a financial coordinator. Sheer efficiency will reign. The financial coordinators will spend 100 percent of their time doing nothing but collecting data and closing sales.

Customer service is another important function that will be taken out of the hands of the financial coordinators in the field. Their job is to sell. They make no house calls. They do no prospecting. They have no responsibility for customer service. Again, a specialized head office team is used for all customer service needs. Those consumers in the 1990s who are comfortable with the use of computers can tap into the head office customer service department electronically and even bridge over to the particular product carrier for specific up-to-date information. The customer service team also may be reached by mail or telephone. Technology will be the key to much that is accomplished at both the head office and field levels of the professional cluster. With so many product suppliers and professional services involved, virtually all customer service will be handled by tapping into various data bases maintained both by the customer service team and the various product and service suppliers. Through these linkages, information can be supplied instantly, directly to the home or office personal computer of the client.

All this allows the financial coordinators and, to a certain extent, the partners themselves to have their time free to do what must be done: Sell—sell—sell.

• A MATTER OF VOLUME

It is a strange contrast. We are entering an age of financial services specialization, yet we portray ourselves as providers of total financial planning advice and every conceivable product. Professional clusters will pull it all together in such a way as to allow a high volume of production at the low unit distribution cost which will be mandatory for survival. A team of head office marketing experts will do the prospecting and bring interested, qualified prospects to the threshold. Financial consultants will take the data. Computers tapped into sophisticated data bases will print out the plans and recommendations rapidly and in high volume. Financial coordinators will then close the sale and posture the client for future purchases. Customer service will be handled by a trained clerical staff armed with computers and electronic linkages. The partners will run the business and provide the necessary specialized expertise.

The professional cluster. Some will be small and some will spread their influence throughout the nation.

Whatever the form, they will furnish a valuable service to the American consumer.

Wake up now! This is not Star Wars. This is real and it is near at hand. It may be the way many of you will operate in the near future or it may be just another competitor. However you view it—good or bad—don't just ignore these possibilities. Instead do something vastly more productive. Start now surveying your own talents, strengths, and weaknesses to determine what your role will be in the strange new environment.

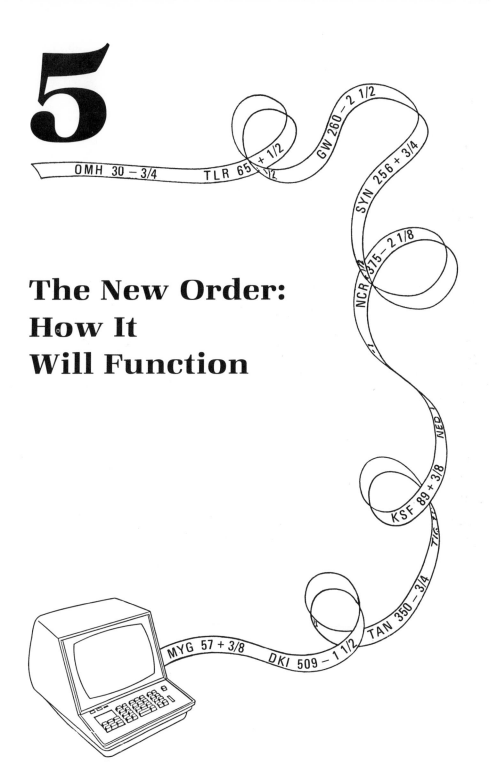

5

OMH 30 – 3/4   TLR 65 + 1/2   GW 260 – 2 1/2   SYN 256 + 3/4   NCR 375 – 2 1/8   NED   KSF 89 + 3/8   TAN 350 – 3/4   MYG 57 + 3/8   DKI 509 – 1 1/2

The New Order:
How It
Will Function

• RUN OUT OF TOWN

I best not mention the event or the city, but it happened just a few years ago. I was nearly run out of town simply for making a few, of what I considered, rather innocent predictions from the podium. In retrospect, it is a wonder I wasn't tarred and feathered, for I was preaching sacrilege to a crowd of rather traditional insurance executives. Their industry hadn't changed much in over one hundred years and they had no intention of making even the slightest of changes now. They were fat and happy, nestled comfortably in the safety of years of undisturbed tranquility. They did not want to hear about any disturbance of the status quo, let alone be subjected to a prediction of revolution.

I guess it was a mutual mistake—theirs for inviting me to be the speaker at their meeting, and mine for both accepting and opening my big mouth in the wrong place. The instance does point up the fact that change within the financial services industry has been occurring at a much more rapid pace during the last three to five years than most of us either realize or care to admit. That point was driven home to me forcefully when, much to my surprise, that very same group of insurance executives recently had me return to their annual meeting, once again as the guest speaker.

Although this time I was billed as "somewhat controversial," I was welcomed with courtesy and eagerness. As I gave them my predictions for the 1990s, they listened attentively and took notes. What had happened to create this radical turnaround in attitude? In just three short years, four of my predictions had already come true and the fifth was beginning to take shape. Suddenly they realized that change was taking place all around them and that they could not avoid it. In self-defense, they wanted to hear more.

Those predictions made three years earlier seem so mundane now. Yet they were radical then. For example, one of the predictions was: "The traditional insurance industry will lose its fight against universal life. The consumer is too smart." Another was: "The insurance industry will launch a mad scramble for alternate, lower-cost distribution systems." Ho-hum material and accepted facts now, but tar and feather material just three years ago. That is how fast change is occurring all around us. It shows every promise of accelerating rapidly during the next five years.

Change itself, and particularly accelerating change, will cause increasing instability within the entire financial services industry. At the recent meeting of those same insurance executives, here is one of the current predictions that I gave them:

> There will be a severe shakeout in the insurance industry—indeed the entire financial services industry—that will leave the whole system permanently restructured. There will be fierce new competition. There will be new distribution systems. Widespread cost cutting will become commonplace. Many companies will not survive. Those that do survive will be changed and there will be sharp distinctions among those survivors.

Radical? I fear not. It may be fact sooner than we'd like to think.

- **FRAGILE FABRIC**

Rapid change creates enormous instability. Most within our industry don't even recognize the change, so the underlying instability remains hidden and becomes as insidious trap for the unwary. One big name financial services corporation recently discovered that fact the hard way.

During the disintermediation of the early 1980s, this particular company faced the rather obvious fact that its existing method of distribution was far too expensive to be a viable delivery system in the future. Therefore, the corporation hired some new, experienced line managers to bring it through the transition. Those new executives decided to accomplish the distribution system streamlining by training the existing field people to be vastly more productive. They laid out a careful plan, built a vision, and, working closely with their key field managers, started making noticeable progress. By the time two years had passed, sales were rising significantly while unit distribution costs were declining. They had built a winning team and they were on the right track for survival and prosperity in the 1990s.

This turnaround, however, was built of a much more fragile fabric than anyone realized, primarily because there still was a mixture of the new and the old. The new was the revitalized distribution system. The old was the traditional, overpowering, nonproductive home office bureaucracy. During the trauma of the changes that were taking place in the field, most of the home office bureaucracy had been hiding in silence, hoping to be overlooked in the changes that were taking place. When they started to see success, however, those home office people felt more secure and thought it was time to get personally involved. And get personally involved they did. As a result, the decision making authority was removed from the line managers and placed in the hands of a network of committees. The obvious result was that all progress stopped. In addition, the timidity of committees in general caused the overturning of decisions that had already been made by the line managers. In just two short calendar quarters all that had been built in the previous two years was destroyed. The field force had accepted many of the changes on faith, but when the committees started to renege on promises all credibility was lost. The spell was broken.

Those home office people who dared not get involved until the very last minute still don't know what happened. Now they sit in their committees, speaking of shutting down that division completely. So far it doesn't seem to have occurred to those executives what will happen to their own jobs if they allow the division to fail.

The point of this example is obvious. In a time of rapid change no company can afford to cling to the old ways and remain static. One must move forward or fall precipitously backwards. Many will learn too late.

• FANNING THE FLAMES

During the next five years things will change even faster, creating more instability. It is almost like a chain reaction, starting almost passively but increasing in speed until it is explosive in character. Between now and the early 1990s powerful new competitors will arrive upon the scene. The financial services conglomerates will finally get their act together, evolve into Generalists, and make a full court press on the upscale consumer market. Banks and the Merchandisers will use their financial service centers to wrap their arms around middle America in an attempt to totally capture that large and lucrative market. The Discounters will use direct response and telemarketing to spread no-load and low-load products of all types throughout the American marketplace. Even the futuristic science of electronic marketing will be silently cutting a wide swath, totally bypassing traditional delivery systems.

As if all of that is not enough, all of the new competition will be fed and even encouraged by a whole new generation of consumers: the so-called baby boomers. That huge segment of the population born between 1946 and 1965 will fan the flames of the financial services revolution. By 1990 this new generation will be coming into their prime. They will be different—much different—from any consumer we have ever faced or even imagined. Although we have discussed them previously, let me summarize their characteristics here because they will be a major factor in completely changing the financial services world as we know it today.

The baby boomers will have more disposable income than any generation in the history of the world. Most households will be headed by two working adults, each with an independent career. They will be tough customers to deal with because they will have a "prove it to me" attitude. They will tend to have less trust in existing institutions, including government at all levels. For example, knowing that there will be a smaller population behind them to fund government transfer programs, they will have very little faith in the Social Security system. As a result, there will be a strong tendency in the financial services arena for them to put less stress on such items as protection or insurance and much more importance on the accumulation of assets for themselves. That will not, however, make them any easier for us to deal with. They will have less trust in financial institutions also. They will have less loyalty. They will demand low cost and high value. They will be much more sophisticated financially and will tend to shop and bargain for all financial services and products. To complicate things even further, they will be computer literate—comfortable in dealing via computer networks both from their offices and from their homes. In fact, to save time in their busy lives, that is exactly what they will do.

• THE GAUNTLET

By now you should be ready to step over the brink, strong enough to face future shock head-on and wise enough to understand the functioning of the strange, new environment of the 1990s.

Your choices soon will become clear: total extinction, mere survival, or newfound prosperity. The gauntlet is about to be thrown, yet most people associated with the financial services industry—from the supplier level through the delivery systems—remain totally unaware. You cannot make your choices in a vacuum. Heed the warning signs and get ready to take action.

You are about to gain one significant advantage over your unsuspecting peers. Soon you will see the foreign, new financial services world of the immediate future spring into life. As the picture develops you will be able to feel it, touch it, live it, and begin to carve out a future for yourself in the vastly altered environment.

This is the financial services world as it will exist and function after Armageddon—after the revolution. It is where you will have to live during the coming decade. Find a home for yourself.

• A NARROWING FIELD

Fairly soon, possibly within as short a time as four to six years, there will exist only five categories of companies which will serve as suppliers of financial services and products. How will they deliver their products to the consumer? Which of the seven surviving delivery systems will each utilize? Marrying the suppliers to their distribution methods in a matrix sets the entire new industry in motion right before your very eyes.

Stop for a moment now to examine the "Financial Services Marketing in the 1990s" chart. On the left, listed vertically, are the five types of suppliers which will evolve as the heart of our industry during the 1990s. Listed across the top, horizontally, are the seven delivery

FINANCIAL SERVICES MARKETING IN THE 1990s

Suppliers / Products and Services	Delivery Systems						
	Independents	Networks	Captives	Financial Centers	Direct Response	Video-tex	Indirect
Wholesalers							
Discounters							
Merchandisers							
Generalists							
Vendors							

systems that will be used by these suppliers to distribute their products and services to their respective markets. Purposely, I have not yet filled in any of the boxes so that you may draw your own conclusions and match each supplier with its most appropriate distribution system.

As you go through this exercise, the methods of future distribution become clear as suppliers are assigned a primary, secondary and, when appropriate, incidental delivery system. Do it now, before you move on. While going through the same exercise myself, I made some rather startling discoveries. By finding them yourself, they will be more clearly embedded in your consciousness. This is the time to fortify yourself for the vital task of preparing your own battle plans for the future.

As you complete the important exercise of filling in the chart, one thing will start to become crystal clear to you. Both in manufacturing and distributing, there will be a narrowing field within the financial services industry. Specialization and highly targeted markets will be the order of the day. Some combinations of suppliers and their primary delivery systems threaten to be so effective as to engulf entire targeted customer groups.

Are you finished now? Do you have each supplier matched with at least its own unique primary delivery system? Now look at it carefully. Where do you fit in? If, somehow, as you completed the matrix, you didn't seem to identify a place in the new order either for yourself or your organization perhaps it was no accident. Change your modus operandi. For every danger exposed by the matrix, multiple opportunities were uncovered.

- **THE NEW ORDER: HOW IT WILL FUNCTION**

Let's start by taking each supplier category in turn, exploring the primary delivery system that each will depend on to deliver its products and/or services to the consumer. Vendors is an interesting place to begin. In terms of the number of new supplier firms that will join the financial services business, the Discounters and the Vendors categories will be the fastest growing suppliers. Additionally, Vendors is unique because it is the only category that supplies only services or service-related products, but actually takes no financial services product as such to the marketplace.

With the many changes taking place in technology, the need for Vendors will be wider than the imagination can reach at this point. All types of computer software will be in demand, ranging from management systems through accounting procedures, sales programs, financial planning, tax planning and problem solving, etc. Third party administrators of employee benefit plans fall into this category, as do the many consulting firms which are springing up to assist financial services companies in avoiding the pitfalls of the financial services revolution. With more and more use of the personal computer linked to outside services via telephone modem, data bases of all types will be in increasing demand. Electronic marketing services are in their infancy at this point, but will constitute a major demand soon.

On the surface, Vendors provide only a service and, hence, seem to pose no threat to any existing distribution system. Take another look. Depending on your point of view, Vendors can be a huge threat to existing distribution systems or, conversely, provide a needed service for many consumers. As just one example, think about individuals who are interested in investing in the stock market. The problem with the stock market is that very few people have ever made any money in a "buy and hold" position. In fact, merely to break even with where the Dow Jones stood twenty years ago on an inflation adjusted basis, the Dow today would have to be well above 3,000. Conclusion? At least during the last twenty years, you had to be a good "trader" to make money in equities. Now, simply add through a Vendor's data base a good market timing service, and now what possibilities do you have? Using the market timing data base, the customer could then save money by dealing with a discount broker. A heavy trader, in fact, could pay for the cost of the personal computer and the data base simply by the commissions saved in dealing with a good discount broker. Now, does this present a threat to stockbrokers who specialize in stock trading accounts? Indeed it does. Using your imagination, you can expand that example one thousand times or more to see where threats to other distributors might pop up.

As a primary delivery system, however, it is obvious that the Vendors will choose the Indirect delivery system for marketing their products. At least initially, most of their customers will be other financial services firms and marketing organizations which need the services of the Vendors. So far you are making a perfect score if you checked "Indirect" as the primary delivery system for Vendors. Keep in mind, however, that when we get to secondary distribution systems we will discover that the Vendors increasingly will go direct to the public through such outlets as Videotex. In the 1990s, in fact, this direct access to the public as an outlet may rival its volume of Indirect services to financial services firms.

As mentioned earlier, the Generalists are characterized by the fact that they handle a full spectrum of financial products and are the only type of supplier in the future that will be able to afford a full-time, career sales force. Think about that for a moment. Does that indicate some changes in the works? Think about the many types of firms that now depend on a so-called captive sales distribution system: stockbrokerages, life insurance companies, direct writing property and casualty companies, mutual fund underwriters, and many more. If it is true that only the Generalists will have a captive distribution system, then what will happen to all these other types of companies? The answer is easy: They will change. Many are already changing.

Those companies who now have full-time sales forces, yet are not in the Generalists category, must do one of two things to survive into the 1990s. If, through expansion or brokerage, they can expand their product lines, and if they can train their field force to handle these new products along with the present ones, they can

FINANCIAL SERVICES MARKETING IN THE 1990s

Delivery Systems

Suppliers Products and Services	Independents	Networks	Captives	Financial Centers	Direct Response	Videotex	Indirect
Wholesalers							★★★
Discounters					★★★		
Merchandisers				★★★			
Generalists			★★★				
Vendors							★★★

evolve into the Generalists category. With the coming squeeze on product profit margins, each salesperson will have to operate at a productivity level previously thought impossible. Only by providing a myriad of products to the customer base can it be accomplished by most companies. Although the exception rather than the rule, there will be a few companies which will remain as specialists in a narrow product line yet maintain a Captive field force. They will accomplish it by combining greatly enhanced field productivity with a product line which provides ample margins to allow such personalized field services. By and large, however, the Captives of the future will be associated with Generalists.

Other than size, the distinctions among the members of the Generalist family will gradually disappear. The unique images of various stockbrokerages and insurance companies will dull as they migrate through the 1990s. A Generalist will be a Generalist, not just an insurance company or a stockbrokerage. All offering a full spectrum of financial products and services, they will tend to look alike. Although a few wise niche marketers will find specialized audiences for their wares, most Generalists will have the identical target in their sights: the capturing of the upscale, affluent consumer market.

If you have not done so already, mark "Captives" as the primary delivery system for the Generalists.

- **YOU CAN BANK ON IT**

Survey after survey have shown that an impressive percentage of American consumers, particularly the emerging baby boomers, are quite comfortable with the "one-stop shopping" approach being set forth by the Merchandisers. We are becoming a busier society, less willing to spend our precious time jumping from one place to another to get our "shopping list" completed. The advent of the modern shopping center has proved the point. Now such gutsy pioneers as Sears are spreading the concept, with considerable success, into the financial services arena. They are rapidly being followed by many others, including the banks. By 1990 virtually all national merchandising organizations that tend to draw a crowd of people regularly to a store or any central location will, at least to some extent, be in the financial services business.

Quite obviously, the primary delivery system for the Merchandisers is found in the "Financial Centers." Middle-income America, in particular, is responding enthusiastically. In these modern times when each partner in a marriage has an independent career, efficiency in shopping becomes a primary item. Generally each individual assumes regular duties, but in many cases for recreation and compatibility purposes these couples will shop together for the important items. A Tuesday evening can become quite productive if you can take the lawn mower in for repairs, buy a new suit, stock up on groceries, and start an IRA account—all in the same store. Sears has been proving for years that this will work with its Allstate Insurance, and now it is just a matter of adding the full spectrum of financial services that can be provided by subsidiaries such as Dean Witter and Coldwell Banker.

Even those Merchandisers who do not have all the subsidiaries of a giant like Sears can get in the act by rounding out their product line through the use of Wholesalers. That, in fact, is how the banks are starting. Actually, at this point, the banks do not qualify as Merchandisers themselves because they manufacture no products whatsoever. They are simply opening financial centers (as well as experimenting with direct response) by making arrangements with other product suppliers. For example, looking at the chart, you can trace what the banks are doing now by assuming that a Wholesaler is providing the product. From the Wholesaler's point of view, this is an Indirect distribution system. The bank appears on the chart at this time only as a Financial Center delivery system. But that is just the beginning. If somehow the banks are successful in eliminating or circumventing the legislative barriers now preventing them, they will eventually toss our their "partners" and enter the Merchandiser category of supplier. You can bank on it.

At a recent meeting of the American Bankers Association, Mr. Peter Blocklin, a lobbyist for the ABA, talked about the progress that the banking industry was making in bringing about the necessary legislation that will allow them to become manufacturers of financial products. Their primary target at this time is the securities business and they fully expect, within a year or two, to underwrite such securities as revenue bonds and mortgage-backed securities. Additionally, they are making a strong run at the insurance industry despite the fact, as Mr. Blocklin puts it, that "The independent agents are a tough lobby." Describing the encounter between the banking and insurance industries, he went on to state: "When insurance and banking clash they're like two behemoths preparing to make love—both are jockeying so that they are not on the bottom."

Should the banks be granted those insurance underwriting powers and the ability to issue securities, they will be a force to reckon with in the Merchandisers category. That is why it is such a strange anomaly, in my opinion, to watch the insurance industry going hellbent for leather to train the banks to sell insurance through the newly founded financial centers in so many bank lobbies. It would have made just about as much sense for David to have trained Goliath in the use of the sling prior to their meeting on the battlefield.

• **AN ANACHRONISM?**

In a feature story appearing in The Wall Street Journal on January 21, 1985, Mr. Terry Havens, an insurance consultant in Lexington, Kentucky, was quoted as saying: "Commissions are an anachronism in our industry. Our industry is changing for the better, and few people know the revolution has begun." I don't think I would go quite as far as Mr. Havens, but there is no doubt whatsoever that the Discounters represent perhaps the fastest growing segment of the financial services industry. Everybody seems to be getting into the act, ranging from companies searching for new distribution outlets, through large national associations and even credit card companies. Their primary delivery system is Direct Response: bypassing all salespeople and other intermediaries by going directly to the public. Their techniques cover virtually all methods of mass merchandising including coupon advertising, direct mail, telemarketing, payroll deduction, and electronic marketing. Many companies will be joining the ranks of the Discounters, and before the end of the decade, virtually every financial services product will be involved.

Many factors are coming together simultaneously to encourage the flourishing of all methods of financial services discounting. Increased competition tends to drive prices down, so the Discounters try to alleviate that problem by eliminating commissions entirely. A better educated and more sophisticated consumer is demanding financial products with less loading for commissions and administrative expenses. Financial services companies, currently desperate to find lower-cost methods of distribution, will be turning to discounting in record numbers in an attempt to eliminate their cost overrun problems.

By 1990 there will be a dog-eat-dog world which will coincide nicely with the maturing of the baby boom generation. The baby boomers are shrewd, financially sophisticated, and they love to shop and bargain. In some respects, the financial services industry of the 1990s may resemble Revolución Boulevard in downtown Tijuana. Consumers may roam from one Discounter to another, making ridiculously low bids and enjoying the crush of counteroffers that are made. At last they will settle on some "special deal," silently hoping that the merchandise will not turn green in the morning.

It is not too early in our discovery process to begin pondering what the secondary delivery system of the Discounters might be. The possibilities are either exciting or chilling, depending on which side of the fence you reside. We will explore them later.

• TRIAL AND ERROR

It's forming almost inadvertently; almost by default. Financial services suppliers are realizing that two major distribution trends are gradually overwhelming them: The financial difficulty of maintaining any type of career sales force without huge gains in productivity, and the resulting need to move larger blocks of product at lower unit cost. Some companies are attacking the problem head-on, providing the leadership that is needed to achieve those productivity gains through their present field forces. Many others, however, have instead begun to search for new methods of delivering their products to the consumer. Many would like to become Generalists, but they feel that they have neither the breadth nor the talents necessary to distribute foreign product lines. Others look longingly at the Merchandisers, but they are not in the type of business in which they can provide retail outlets for financial services side by side with unrelated products. Some are trying to back into that category by making arrangements with banks, but for most that experiment may be destined for bitter disappointment. Other established companies are toying with the idea of becoming Discounters, but most are doing it halfheartedly because years of tradition have ingrained in their minds the belief that discounting financial services products somehow borders on immorality. So they just sort of back into the only other alternative available—they are becoming Wholesalers.

The majority of existing financial services companies —at least those that survive the revolution—will end up in the Wholesaler category whether they intend to or not. The Wholesalers are those suppliers which manufacture products only and control no delivery system which goes directly to the public. In today's terminology, the Wholesalers parallel what most of us would refer to as the brokerage business. They manufacture products and attempt to distribute or broker those products through uncontrolled delivery systems, such as independent agents, unattached registered representatives, and financial planners. This form of distribution will change drastically in the 1990s, but currently examples of Wholesalers would be the traditional property and casualty companies (other than the direct writers), NASD dealers who provide products only but who do not finance registered representatives, and the many life insurance companies who attempt to distribute through independent general agents. The primary delivery system for Wholesalers, therefore, is Indirect.

Why, then, didn't I call this category "brokerage"? Because, like so many other things in the financial services industry, the tactics employed by these types of companies will change drastically during the revolution. As mentioned earlier, the key to survival will be moving product in volume while maintaining very low distribution costs. You cannot do that by dealing one-on-one with independent producers and small shops.

How, then, can you move product in volume without controlling any distribution system? By going through the established outlets of others. Arrangements of these types are already being put together. For example, there are many of what I refer to as "boutique" manufacturers who specialize in manufacturing just one line of products. By concentrating on just one product or a family of closely related products, the manufacturer then attempts to be the very best in that narrow field. This type of Wholesaler then makes arrangements with others, such as a Generalist, to provide that particular product through the Generalist's distribution system. These types of products, from the Generalist's point of view, do not generally represent a major product line but do represent the kind of product they need to round out their portfolio. It would be too expensive to develop a minor product line themselves, so they are content to enter into an agreement to sell that particular product manufactured by the Wholesaler. Many of these types of arrangements involve what I call a "phantom supplier": a Wholesaler who manufactures the product using the private label of the larger company which controls the distribution system.

Wholesalers in the next few years will develop other

types of imaginative outlets for their products, such as franchising agreements with Networks and distributing through the use of intermediary marketing groups. Remember my mention of some friends who left a major NYSE member firm to set up such an intermediary marketing group? Their technique has been to go to various product suppliers, such as insurance companies, with the premise that if those companies will develop a specialized type of product and give them an exclusive marketing agreement, this marketing group would take that product to various NYSE member firms for distribution. Working on volume, such intermediaries can afford to work on a very small markup, thereby lowering the distribution cost of the Wholesaler. From the point of view of the stockbrokerage firm, these individuals do provide a specialized marketing expertise at no cost to the firm. Regardless of the distribution method employed, the key to success is wholesaling: moving product in volume at small markup. Existing supplier companies that have the foresight to be worrying about survival at this time would be well-advised to explore the opportunities of wholesaling. The techniques are rather new and require imagination, but the opportunities are boundless.

• DISCOVERY

And now you have it. The picture is starting to form. You have identified all of the primary delivery systems of the suppliers of the future. Wholesalers and Vendors will use Indirect delivery methods. Discounters will concentrate predominantly on Direct Response. Merchandisers will make inroads through their Financial Centers. The Generalists will be the only type of supplier maintaining a full-time, career distribution system and they will use their Captives to the utmost in their attempt to dominate the affluent market.

It is fascinating to observe the mad scramble going on now in the financial services industry. A few of the aggressive, forward thinking firms already know exactly where they are going within this matrix and they are relentlessly, yet silently, laying the groundwork to become a major force in the niche they have selected. The majority of financial services companies, particularly those steeped in tradition, are still floundering in confusion. In the prosperity of recent years, mapping changes in strategic directions has not been a burden that they have had to wrestle with. They are afraid, yet frozen in indecision. Somehow they had better find a way to break that awful spell or they will find themselves still standing in confusion when the waves of defeat come crashing down. There is very little time left.

It is time once again in our exercise to stop, examine, and analyze. We have made a major step forward. We have studied the five supplier categories of the future in relation to the seven delivery systems which will exist in the 1990s. More specifically, we have identified the four delivery systems which will be the primary supplier outlets for distributing financial services and products to the various consumer markets: Captives, Financial Centers, Direct Response and Indirect.

If you will remember, I stated earlier that in putting together this financial services matrix I made a few rather startling discoveries. Enough of the pieces of the puzzle are now in place where at least one of those discoveries should be jumping out at you and screaming: "Look at me! There is an apparent anomaly here. Is something wrong or are we on the brink of a major discovery? I am the matrix. I am your friend. I am trying to tell you something! We have discovered that no one—I repeat, not one supplier—has selected Independents as a primary distribution system!"

When I first discovered that fact it puzzled me greatly. After I thought about it a bit, the reasons finally came into focus. As I mentioned earlier, the survival of Independents is in great danger for several reasons. From a practical standpoint, the costs of operating as an Independent are entirely too high. With the shrinking product margins, it will be difficult for any individual producers to survive alone unless they have a very select clientele which can support them on fees alone. But there are other reasons why even the independent, fee-based practices may have problems. With the advent of the technological advances of this decade, the availability to nationwide data bases and computer networks will be a necessity not only for retrieving and assembling data, but also for such things as contacting clients, executing orders, and staying up-to-date on the fast moving product environment which will operate mainly by computer. The sheer cost of having access to such linkages may be prohibitive except for the most productive insurance agents, financial planners, and independent registered representatives. Now pile on just one other factor: the availability of product. Only the Wholesaler type of supplier will be willing to provide product to Independents, but their objective will be to move large amounts of product through few distribution systems. Most will not waste time dealing with the low volume units that most independent producers represent. Without banding together into Networks, most Independents will find themselves in deep financial trouble and starved for product lines.

That, of course, is why it is so ironic to see so many present day financial services companies diving headlong into the competition to make independent producers a primary distribution system. The life insurance companies are providing the greatest spectacle. Because of the high cost of their traditional agency systems, they are abandoning their career sales forces and attempting to romance the many newly created independent general agents and personally producing general agents. With the majority of the life insurance companies in the United States taking this same route simultaneously, the competition is driving distribution costs up, not down. This, of course, flies in the face of all the trends toward lower costs, efficiency, and productivity. The implosion is coming. Most so-called Independents will be forced out of business. Those wise enough to see it coming in advance will form Networks which will, at least to a great extent, preserve their independence of operation.

By now you should be mumbling to yourself: "Now I've got him. He's pushing Networks, yet our Financial Services 1990 Matrix indicated that no one would have Networks as a primary distribution system. How is he going to wriggle out of this one?" Good question. You have, in fact, identified one of the primary reasons why Networking will be absolutely necessary in the 1990s. All suppliers will have a mass-merchandising bias. They will refuse to deal with small outlets. The Generalists will have their Captive systems and the other suppliers will be looking for similar collective distribution clout. Only by networking will previously independent agents, financial planners, and registered reps have the necessary purchasing power to get the attention of the Wholesalers. Oh, yes, it will be primarily the Wholesalers who serve the Networks, but, conversely, Networks will never be the primary distribution system for Wholesalers. The larger the Network, therefore, the more attention it can demand. As mentioned earlier, there will be many forms of Networks, ranging from informal cooperatives to highly structured organizations. However it is accomplished, one thing is clear: The Independents of the future will have to Network, or they may be out of business.

• THE REST OF THE STORY

We've already started to progress beyond looking solely at primary delivery systems, so let's go the rest of the way and fill in the remaining pieces of the puzzle. In fact, as we complete the matrix, you may find a few more surprises in store. As we fill in the chart, marking both secondary supplier outlets and incidental delivery methods, we see certain other patterns start to form.

First, let's look again at the Wholesalers. As discussed earlier, Indirect delivery methods will be their primary concentration because that will be the only way they can move large amounts of merchandise at a relatively low distribution cost. Their secondary outlet, however, will indeed be the Networks. In fact, as Networks start to form and grow, they will represent a significant secondary outlet for Wholesalers. Many companies in the Wholesaler category are going to find themselves in trouble. When they realize that dealing with so-called Independents is driving their distribution costs up, they may abandon their Independents entirely. Those who do so without already having their Indirect outlets (such as phantom supplier arrangements) set up will find themselves virtually out of business. The smart Wholesalers with foresight, therefore, should now be working not only on forming their Indirect distribution systems, but also on encouraging the formation of Networks. Some companies will find themselves in a leadership position if they start now bringing Independents together into formal Networks for the mutual prosperity of both those Networks and their Wholesaler partners. From the point of view of the Networks themselves, the bigger the Network and the more organized it is, the better chance it will have of playing a key role in the future. In an era of mass-merchandising preferences, bargaining power will be essential.

As we study the rest of the completed matrix, the addition of secondary and incidental supplier outlets starts to form some new patterns. For example, it starts to become obvious that there will be a good bit of experimentation with direct response selling by 1990. The Discounters will not be alone in their search for high volume, low cost, and improved productivity. After all, it makes sense that Sears would not ignore their millions of credit card customers. Although its primary outlets will be Financial Centers, Sears could very easily direct mail financial services to their credit card holders much as it does now with other types of merchandise via its catalog operation. This could even be done in such a manner as not to conflict with its Financial Centers by selecting noncompetitive geographical locations and income groups. Some of the larger Generalists, such as American Express, will have identical thoughts. It would not be prudent for them to ignore that credit card base which

FINANCIAL SERVICES MARKETING IN THE 1990s

Suppliers / Products and Services	Delivery Systems						
	Independents	Networks	Captives	Financial Centers	Direct Response	Video-tex	Indirect
Wholesalers	•	◆◆				•	★★★
Discounters		•			★★★	◆◆	
Merchandisers				★★★	•	◆◆	
Generalists			★★★		•	◆◆	
Vendors	•	•			•	◆◆	★★★

Supplier outlets: ★★★ Primary ◆◆ Secondary • Incidental

represents virtually millions of potential financial services clients.

So much talk of direct response rightly rankles the
true professionals in our industry. Just what is the magic
appeal of going directly to the customer? The individual
stockbrokers, agents, financial planners and other
salespeople have, for years, served the customer well by
offering personalized, tailored advice and recommendations. Why cheapen the industry by circumventing these
professionals entirely and trying to deal directly with the
customer? The answer lies not in preference, but in hard
economics and the law of supply and demand. You cannot
fight the trend of the times. Although there will always be
customers who need, want and are willing to pay for
tailored advice, a growing segment of the population is
leaning more and more toward convenience and price in
all of their shopping, including financial services.

Most of the current success stories in the financial
services business, in fact, center around Discounters.
We've already discussed the amazing growth of the discount stockbrokerage business. Additionally, the no-load
mutual funds for years have made inroads to the extent
that they now dominate their business. Others are on the
way, such as companies like USAA of San Antonio, Texas.
They represent an interesting story. Originally, the company was founded just to provide automobile insurance
for officers of the armed forces. All of their business was
done by mail exclusively with that targeted clientele.
Over the years, they have expanded greatly, even adding
telemarketing skills to their direct mail operations. They
are willing to take risks and will enter a market, if
necessary, by controlled trial and error until they make it
work. A recent example was their entrance into the direct
mail life insurance business. At first, they stumbled and
bumbled. Most of the rest of us in the industry said: "I
told you so. You can't sell life insurance by direct mail."
Trial and error. Determination and marketing skill. They
did put it together. Today they sell 75,000 universal life
policies a year, totally by direct mail with telemarketing
follow-up.

Now what is the appeal of all this? Productivity. Up until recently, it was considered a major accomplishment for a life insurance agent to sell a million dollars worth of insurance in a single calendar year. Now much higher standards of productivity are becoming commonplace. At USAA they require their agents (who work via telemarketing) to shoot for $100 million in annual sales in order to be considered productive. That, in a nutshell, is the appeal of discounting to the boards of directors of companies reeling under the pressures of high overhead cost and looking for more effective ways to stay in business.

Regardless of which supplier category and distribution system you may be associated with, the secret of continued success into the 1990s keeps boiling down to one thing: greatly enhanced productivity. Whether the member of a Captive distribution system, a sole proprietor producer, or part of a home office team, new standards of excellence will be expected of each of us.

Study the matrix. Read and understand what it is trying to tell you. Compare our industry of tomorrow with your present responsibilities. Whether you presently are a professional salesperson, teacher, trainer, clerk, or top executive, do you fit with the radical new order which will exist after the revolution? If yes, then fortify your position and be a leader into this battle. If you or your organization, however, do not mesh with the future, then take steps to change things immediately. There will be no mercy shown and no prisoners taken if the financial services revolution materializes as fast as I fear it might.

• A TSUNAMI

No, I did not overlook it. How could I? It is the most dramatic discovery uncovered by our Financial Services 1990 chart. It is the sleeper that will revolutionize our lives. At this very moment, in fact, the smart money—big money—is working relentlessly, yet silently, to explode this one in our faces, perhaps before the end of the current decade.

It is so obvious now. Yet it remains so deeply submerged. There is no doubt that this is the most powerful tidal wave of all, racing toward its nearby destination with alarming speed. Few see it yet. Many will be overwhelmed.

The matrix exposes only one delivery system which will be utilized by *all* of the suppliers: Videotex. It jumps out at us, screaming to be recognized. Along with its dangers, it promises an entirely new spectrum of opportunity for adventuresome practitioners and a new world of freedom for consumers.

6

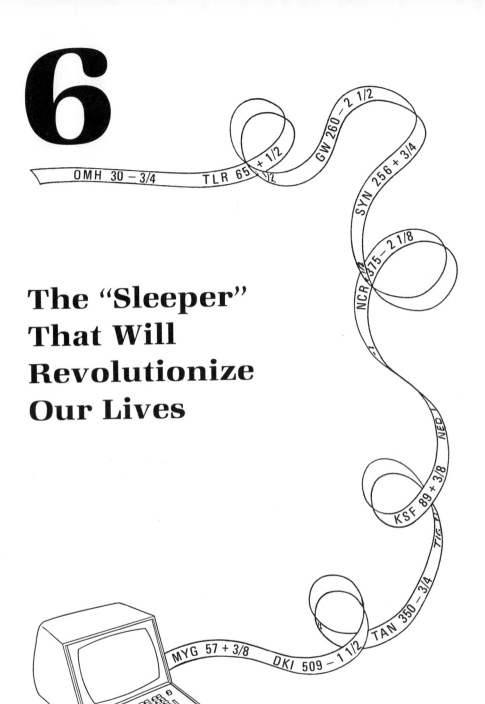

The "Sleeper" That Will Revolutionize Our Lives

• RUNNING FREE

Let's look way out into the future for a moment. Maybe beyond the year 2,000. If you are a salesperson of financial products, don't let this next exercise threaten you. By the time it could materialize to the extent presented, you will have adjusted to the new environment. As you can see, even though the interview technique has been altered, the basic sales process remains the same. Whether in person or electronically (or, most likely, a combination of the two), you remain at stage center. Despite the wave of new technology and the entrance of new types of competitors, you will remain the catalyst which keeps our industry moving. The electronic revolution, in fact, may be the tool that carries you triumphantly through the financial services revolution. Let's survey available technology, interpret present-day trends and let our minds and imaginations run free.

• KISS THE BABY

With squeezed commissions, lower margins, and higher operating costs, how will the salespersons of the future be able to afford the time for one-on-one, face-to-face sales presentations? Perhaps they won't, except for their most affluent customers and in special markets that call for personal service. There will be a more efficient way.

Most of it will be done in the clients' homes or offices via a two-way cable TV/computer arrangement known as Videotex. The financial coordinators of professional clusters, for example, will arrange appointments for client presentations via telephone or computer. At the selected time, the client will switch on his television set and activate his computer. The presentation will be made, questions and answers handled, data transmitted and transactions executed from perhaps hundreds of miles away. The necessity for a personal sales call will diminish.

Gone will be the typical life insurance person of the past who made most sales at night in the prospect's home. The sheer inefficiency of the practice limited sales opportunities to one, or at the most two, per day. Think of it: You drive twenty miles to the appointment, ring the bell, shake hands, settle down with small talk, and finally make the presentation. Then you drink a cup of coffee, eat some pie, kiss the baby, shake hands, get in your car, and drive home. It was fun, perhaps, but it is a rapidly disappearing art. Kiss it goodbye. In the same time frame you now can be making ten presentations electronically.

• THE BABY BOOMERS

If electronic marketing sounds far-fetched to some of you veterans, you'd better talk to your kids before you discard the idea. For example, 12 percent of all teenagers now own a home computer! The number is growing rapidly. Turning to the young adult market, over 22 percent of baby boom generation households either now own a personal computer or plan to buy one in the immediate future. That number will rise rapidly because they have been taught to feel comfortable with the "user friendly" technology and they appreciate its efficiency.

On a rudimentary basis, two-way electronic communication in the home is already in full swing. A friend of mine (one of the older generation, in fact) owns a computer, printer, and telephone modem to follow the stock market and execute transactions. He is one of the 200,000 subscribers to the Dow Jones News/Retrieval data base and he uses that connection each evening to survey the latest news releases and financial updates on his favorite stocks. After surveying the current information, he makes his decisions and actually leaves a trade order for his broker to execute at the market opening in the morning. All this from the comfort of his home.

But that is not all. Some of the other activity he has uncovered over the wires is amazing. A psychologist, for example, takes questions from patients in the evening via computer. After offering his professional advice, he engages in some electronic dialog with the patient. When that avenue is exhausted, he then asks other listening participants for their comments. Participants may then make their contributions by entering their comments on their own keyboards and during the entire process all participants retain their anonymity. When the session is over, the patient is billed electronically for the doctor's time.

And that is just the beginning. It is here today and it is here to stay.

• THE STATE OF THE ART

When our 1990s Financial Services Matrix matched the suppliers with the various delivery systems, Videotex leaped out as the only product and service distribution method which would be utilized in some way by every supplier category. It is no wonder. Think of the flexibility and sheer efficiency of it.

In its simplest sense, Videotex is any information service that gets data from and sends messages to a central computer. The secret is two-way, computer-linked communications directly from the home. There are three primary components: a central computer with various data bases, any interactive communications network for transmitting data (such as telephone or cable TV), and a user terminal (usually a personal computer with its screen and printer). If telephone lines are involved, a telephone modem completes the circuit.

Once you have the hardware in place, Videotex can be put to many uses. The first and most obvious is transactions. Directly from the home, the customer can pay bills, transfer funds, make airline reservations and even indulge in some shopping. Videotex can also be used for information retrieval. The users can be linked with various data bases from which they can select material and even make comparisons. The type of information that can be called up ranges from very general newspaper-type items to specialized information selected from an electronic catalog. There are many other uses for Videotex, such as electronic mail, computing (using the programs of the larger, central computer), and even telemonitoring. This last service is one that connects the user's home to the central computer for the purposes of security or such items as energy management. Via this remote hookup, remote sensing for smoke, fire, or even intruders can be carried on instantaneously. Home appliances, ranging from heaters and air conditioners to coffee pots, can also be switched on and off electronically from a remote location.

These types of services are more than just a gleam in some inventor's eye. They have actually existed in Europe since the late 1970s and in the United States since the latter part of 1983. The pioneer in the United States was Knight-Ridder Newspapers' Viewtron system, which was introduced to subscribers in the Miami, Florida area. Since that time, Knight-Ridder has been joined by such prestigious names as Dow Jones, H & R Block (CompuServe, Inc.), Times Mirror (their Gateway Service in Orange County, California), and Reader's Digest (The Source).

So far, Videotex has been relatively slow to catch on, primarily because of the lack of sufficient hardware (either personal computers or dedicated terminals) in the home. With the rapid growth of the availability of that hardware, however, other prestigious firms are starting to get involved. Associated in one way or another with Videotex are such additional prestigious names as Citibank, Chemical Bank, Chase Manhattan, Bank of America, Merrill Lynch, E F Hutton, and Equitable Life. Many of these players in this new marketplace are comparing the development of Videotex with the growth of such innovations as television, the automobile, and even the telephone. It took years for them to get off the ground and to be accepted, but when they reached a certain stage they nearly exploded in growth and changed our lives forever. In the financial services industry, Videotex is definitely the "sleeper" that will revolutionize our professional lives.

• THE $450 MILLION BET

The management consulting firm of Booz Allen & Hamilton has predicted that by the mid-1990s as many as thirty million households will do nearly $60 billion of shopping via Videotex. The financial services arena is shaping up to be one of the largest Videotex markets. Three corporate giants are betting a minimum of $450 million that it is true. IBM, Sears, and CBS have formed a joint venture that will provide nationwide Videotex services as early as 1987. Their new company will be called Trintex and, for the first time, it brings a wide diversity of skills to the marketplace in one nationwide venture. CBS knows how to develop and market both information and entertainment. IBM is not only a prime maker of computer hardware, but is also a leading supplier of software, and has experience in sophisticated data base networks. Sears, of course, has a huge customer base, proven marketing talents, and the retail units of Dean Witter, Allstate Insurance and Coldwell Banker.

What is it they are betting on? Already there are over ten million American homes that are equipped with personal computers and the growth is continuing at an amazing pace. These firms, therefore, want to join the many others who are getting in position to be at the leading edge of this new phenomenon called Videotex. Mr. W. W. Seelinger of IBM put it this way: "Videotex is the way a majority of the people will first put their hands on and use a computer-related device—both at home and at work—which will result in a major behavioral and cultural change in our society."

CBS, IBM, and Sears know that the consumer of the 1990s will have experienced the pervasiveness of the computer in virtually every aspect of his or her life. He or she will have begun to expect a certain level of electronic efficiency in all business and personal affairs. By now it is second nature to use a personal computer for bill paying, electronic mail and other communications, information storage, and even research. Punch a few buttons and you can call up a program to accomplish almost anything. There is a comfort level with computers, particularly when a visual display, upon command, can personalize a transaction.

- **THE SNOWBALL**

Heard enough? Convinced yet? If not, put these additional facts in your pipe and smoke them. In June 1985 another formidable joint venture in Videotex was announced, this time involving Chemical Bank, Bank of America, American Telephone & Telegraph, and Time, Inc. Already in full swing, initially it offered computerized banking, discount stockbrokerage and merchandise shopping. Targeted services for the future? You guessed it. As they described it: "expanded financial management." That's your market and they are after it. So are RCA and Citicorp, another announced Videotex partnership. It's starting to snowball.

By the early 1990s, much of what we have formerly considered personal financial affairs will be carried on via computer, sometimes from the office but mostly from home. Such financial recommendations may be received over computer either via confidential transmittal on the printer or via visual presentation. Products will be un-bundled and dissimilar products seemingly combined. When a recommendation is made involving the products of many different companies, it can appear as one product with one electronic billing through a single servicing agency. The whole package can be administered automatically for a fee or, if preferred, tracked by the consumer with the help of his or her personal computer.

Keep in mind that the technology for doing all of this is already available. The only thing we're discussing now is the use of all that technology which has literally exploded in the last decade or so. The implications for society in general, and financial services in particular, are awesome.

• A WALK INTO THE FUTURE

Click. It is almost imperceptible. You can barely hear it even through the crisp mountain air of Redcliff, Colorado. It is 5:30 A.M. Harry Townsend's personal computer just turned on the coffee pot. At 6:00 A.M. it will monitor both the outside and inside temperatures, then turn up the heat as it senses that these mornings in the month of May can still be chilly in the mountains of Colorado.

Whir. A barely recognizable sound comes from the media room. It's 6:03 A.M. and the computer's printer has started its day. Sometime in the early hours, while Harry slept, his personal computer had made contact with a mainframe program in New York City. The work of the previous day, including Harry's afternoon calculations and recommendations, had been stored in preparation for this moment. The information was transmitted to New York, mixed with the vast resources of the Network's larger program, and, well before 6:00 A.M., the final recommendations were ready for printing. By the time Harry opens his office for the business day, the documents will be completed and ready for his review. Even here in the beauty and serenity of the Rocky Mountains, Wednesday promises to be another busy and productive day.

Harry Townsend does not have to live in the town of Redcliff, Colorado. He is not a miner or a mountaineer. He certainly doesn't manage one of the nearby ski resorts, although he does enjoy a frequent run down their slopes. Harry Townsend is a financial planner. He lives in the mountains of Colorado by choice.

In this enlightened year of 1994, an established professional or a skillful technician can live almost anywhere of his or her choosing. Several years ago, Harry and his wife Marcia made the decision that the quality of life they wanted was rural. Both of them love to ski, so the mountains were an obvious lure. Harry was an established financial planner in Cleveland, but he found himself spending more and more time on his beloved slopes. It was in those mountains, in fact, that he met Marcia, a lawyer practicing corporate law for a large, well-known law firm in Denver.

It was four years ago when they had made the big move. With the advent of electronic communications and the advances of computer technology, both of them felt they could carry on the daily activities of their professions from a remote location. No longer was an individual tied to the exact geographical place of employment or professional activity. So, Harry and Marcia got married and moved to the mountains. At age forty-two, Harry was now a successful financial planner with a large, fairly affluent practice dealing with individuals in the Midwest. Marcia, at age forty, continued her law practice from her office converted from an upstairs bedroom in their home.

6:30 A.M. First, a computerized voice announces the time and temperature. Then, as in the old days, the annoying alarm goes off. Harry drags himself out of bed, pours a cup of freshly brewed coffee and heads for the shower.

By 7:15 A.M. Harry is already tinkering in the media room which he uses for an office. Beginning in the early 1990s, most houses were constructed with a very important, central media room. It replaced the den of the older days, but could still be used for that purpose in the evenings to watch TV or listen to music. During the day, however, the media room served many purposes, ranging from electronic grocery shopping to serving as an office for Harry. The media room was the central location for all electronic functions, ranging from climate control in the house to the personal computer and the entire Videotex system. The oversized, collapsible TV screen could be used for regular television viewing, for Videotex, or the visual display for the personal computer. The media room was the heartbeat—the very circulatory system—of Harry's home and his entire professional life.

Harry settled down behind his desk, punched in an access code and then entered the date. Immediately the computer printed out his "to do" lists for the day, both personal and business. Automatically it then displayed and printed his itinerary for the day, including the calendar and all appointments.

Working from the "to do" lists, Harry first started on his personal chores for the day. He did have to buy a birthday gift for Marcia, but he had already decided what it would be. He called up the appropriate catalog on his personal computer, ordered the gift, paid for it, and gave the delivery date and address. He then checked the roundtrip airline schedules from Denver to Cleveland, scratched his head in thought as he surveyed the display screen, and finally punched the buttons necessary to nail down the desired reservations. To finish up his early morning chores he then, via Videotex, purchased three lottery tickets and instructed the computer to balance his checkbook. The computer obeyed promptly and when it was finished printed out a summary status report on the account. Harry studied the form, looked satisfied, and then turned his attention to business affairs.

A few more entries on the computer and Harry was in business. His first task was to download the electronic mail that his computer had dutifully logged in during the night. Most of it was rather routine correspondence and customer service requests from clients. During the next forty-five minutes, he handled what customer service requirements there were by directly interfacing with the mainframe computers of the various product suppliers involved. When all the requests were sorted and complied with, Harry dictated the various responses. He rather enjoyed this time of his working day, for he answered his mail in conversational tone, simply talking into a microphone which was an integral part of an attachment to his personal computer. The computer would assimilate his voice, automatically take care of the punctuation, and print out the letter for his signature. "The wonders of modern science," Harry mused to himself.

For the rest of the morning, Harry kept his electronic appointments. When he had a conversation with an existing client, Harry could automatically call up the transaction history of that client and the complete current account status. He would make certain recommendations to his clients and, for the most part, they would execute those recommendations electronically. All conversations and all transactions were made a part of the clients' permanent records automatically.

10:00 was a special time for Harry. First, he would check the progress of the stock market. Occasionally, he would execute a buy or a sell over his Videotex system. Then he would retreat for a moment to the kitchen to fix his brunch. Promptly at 10:30 (12:30 P.M. Eastern Time), Harry would initiate his luncheon interview with his potential new customer for the day. It was kind of fun to have lunch electronically. The huge TV screen would show the image of the customer and there would be two-way voice communication. They would get acquainted over lunch and then get down to business. Although the customer might be 1,700 miles away, it was a very personalized luncheon. Harry would, of course, assure the client that all information given to him would be kept in confidence. Harry would then explain the advantages of the services he provided through his financial planning firm. The last three quarters of the hour during the luncheon period generally was devoted to gathering data from the client. Much of the information could be obtained from the client personally. Things such as wills and other important documents would have to be copied and sent either electronically or through the U.S. mail. Harry assured the customer that once all the information was received by him he would immediately start to work on the financial plan for the client. They could not shake hands electronically, but other than that the interview was very personal and quite intimate—yet Harry never left his home. His client never left the faraway office.

The afternoons were rather quiet for Harry. He'd spend the time studying the new information he had received both from clients and from new prospects. Almost every afternoon he worked on putting together his financial plans and client recommendations. Updates would be done first because they generally took very little time. New financial plans took much longer, so Harry would struggle with those during the afternoon. Then about 5:00 P.M. Harry would generally sign out, punching the appropriate terminology into his personal computer. The computer could then rest, other than taking care of such things as electronic mail, the house security system, and the energy management for the entire home and office complex.

• HERE TODAY

The technology discussed above is already in place and functioning. Nothing is "futuristic" about the explanation of Harry Townsend's day. Only a few years had passed and allowed Harry to become more comfortable with the technology that already exists among us.

Videotex, in fact, is merely the combination of existing technologies. You need a mainframe computer and various data bases; you need some sort of communications network, such as cable TV or telephone lines; you need a television set or some sort of visual display screen; and you need some software. All exist today. In fact, virtually all American homes already have both a TV and telephone. All that is really needed to get Videotex under way is the presence of personal computers in more homes.

Videotex started in Europe in the early 1970s and came to the United States eight to ten years later. At that time, the fledgling industry tried to instigate the two-way communications of Videotex via the sale of separate terminals which cost the consumer upwards of $500. That investment, plus a monthly subscription fee, would provide a rather limited array of information and, in some cases, shopping services. Although some Videotex services were successful, up to this point it has been largely a matter of trial and error. But it is starting to catch on now. Dow Jones started its service in the late 1970s. By 1983 they had 60,000 subscribers and reportedly have well in excess of 200,000 subscribers today. CompuServe, which provides shopping and general information, also has in the area of 200,000 subscribers and, reportedly, The Source is approaching 100,000 subscribers. A drop in the bucket, perhaps, but so was TV when compared to radio—initially. That's an interesting analogy, in fact. Radio wasn't destroyed by the advent of TV, but it was altered drastically. We'll see similar alterations in the financial services business.

It was so slow at first. It seemed that the linking and widespread utilization of Videotex technology would never fully materialize. Now, however, it is nearly exploding upon the scene, with new services being announced almost daily. Charles Schwab & Co., the discount brokerage subsidiary of BankAmerica, is selling a new software service for investors with home computers. The service links existing data bases, such as Dow Jones

News/Retrieval and Standard & Poor's MarketScope, as well as providing price quotes. Even on weekends the customer can place buy and sell orders for execution when the market opens Monday morning. H & R Block's CompuServe is jumping into the fray, offering a similar service in connection with Quick & Reilly, Value Line, Standard & Poor's and the Federal Reserve Bank. The examples are countless, with new players joining the race in record numbers.

There have only been two things holding back the more rapid growth of Videotex. The first obstacle has been relatively high fees for the services. Normally, customers pay a sign-up charge (typically $100 or more) and then have to pay "connect time" for each minute the service is used. The second rein on Videotex's growth was the fact, at least in the early days, that the customer additionally had to buy or rent a specialized, dedicated terminal to handle the technology. The fees, in my opinion, will disappear as more customers utilize Videotex and new commercial players enter the scene. Competition for the consumers' attention and dollars has a marvelous way of eliminating unnecessary costs. And the dedicated terminals? They, too, will disappear. Once consumers learn of the many products, services, data bases and other benefits available through the ownership of a home computer, existing personal computers will be utilized for Videotex and new computers will be added to households which, up to now, have been resisting the purchase. What IBM, Sears, CBS, and the others know—and now you and I also know—is that Videotex will soar in popularity when it is tied solely into the personal computer which will reside in the vast majority of households by the mid-1990s.

Trial and error. Start, stumble, learn and rebuild. Most of that is behind the Videotex industry at this point. Now its growth is becoming targeted, with financial services one of the primary thrusts. It is about to become a major factor in our business.

• AN ERA OF FREEDOM

Rather than fear such innovations as Videotex, many forward-thinking players in the financial services world will use the new technology to discover an entirely new era of freedom. It may seem strange to some of you out there, but did you know that there are already over seven million people who are now "telecommuters"? Telecommuters are people who work at home or at some location far removed from the central office, using computers instead of automobiles to commute and communicate with the central office. Seven million people have already discovered its conveniences. Within the next few years, we will see it spread into the financial services business. The need for efficiency will demand it.

Currently, there is a frantic search underway by all major suppliers of financial services and products. The challenge is to find lower cost methods of distribution. Most of them don't realize it yet, but Videotex is the answer for many of them. The technology is already available and in the homes. Videotex is just another service that can be added over the wires. It is nothing more than efficient, computer related, two-way communication. By the year 2000, it will gradually evolve into more than just a secondary delivery system. It will become the primary method of distribution for more than one type of supplier company.

Rather than fear this new technology, stop to think for a moment about the degree of freedom it may introduce into your lives. Whether you are a home office employee or a member of the field distribution system, with responsibilities for directly contacting customers, Videotex unleashes you from the idea that you must be near the central home office or field office location. Think about it: Wouldn't it be much more convenient to spend your commuting time making your life more efficient? Wouldn't you really prefer to work from the comfort of your own home?

The demographic and social implications of Videotex

for the 1990s are great. Already there is a strong trend away from the cities and toward the suburbs. Videotex not only will accelerate this, but will send people far away from those central cities. Everything can be done from the home. Business, shopping, even childrens' education. Yes, there will be a trend away from the central aspect of the education of children. Society may tend to become more antisocial as children and adults alike receive their education, do their shopping, and even conduct their business from their own homes.

No, I'm not predicting an impersonal, totally antisocial society on the other side of the electronic and financial services revolutions. Each of us must recognize, however, that not only will such patterns be possible, but they will in fact be adopted by many. Rather than a threat, I view it more as an additional market that many of you may wish to get ready for. I would anticipate that the majority of people will opt for maintaining more customary social patterns, but keep in mind that even the majority will have considerably more electronic efficiency introduced into their lives.

In 1984, Business Week reported Jonathan S. Beacher as saying: "Our research has found that half the country is planning to buy a personal computer, but when you ask them what they're going to do with it you find a lot of confusion." Mr. Beacher, a Senior Vice President of Reymer & Gersin Associates and a Videotex market researcher, went on to say: "Whoever is the first to sell communications services with home computers will revolutionize the home computer business. That's what it will take to get computers into 60 percent to 70 percent of all households." Videotex is tying it all together.

- **A TIME FOR REFLECTION**

At this particular point, you can have only one of two opposite reactions. First, you can decide that I have finally fallen out of my tree. If that is your reaction, I certainly can understand it. Facing an uncertain future is difficult enough without trying to make such definite predictions. Hopefully, however, you have been stimulated and challenged to explore further how these concepts might impact your professional life.

My advice to you all is to make this a time for thoughtful reflection. Learn and then react. Apply these new thoughts to the supplier category or delivery system where you presently earn your living. See where you fit in. Better yet, see where there may be fantastic opportunities for you if you act now.

John Naisbitt, in his best selling *Megatrends: Ten New Directions Transforming Our Lives,* states: "We are living in the time of the parenthesis, the time between eras. Those who are willing to handle the ambiguity of this in between period and to anticipate the new era will be a quantum leap ahead of those who hold onto the past."

In the financial services industry there is little time left for the old era.

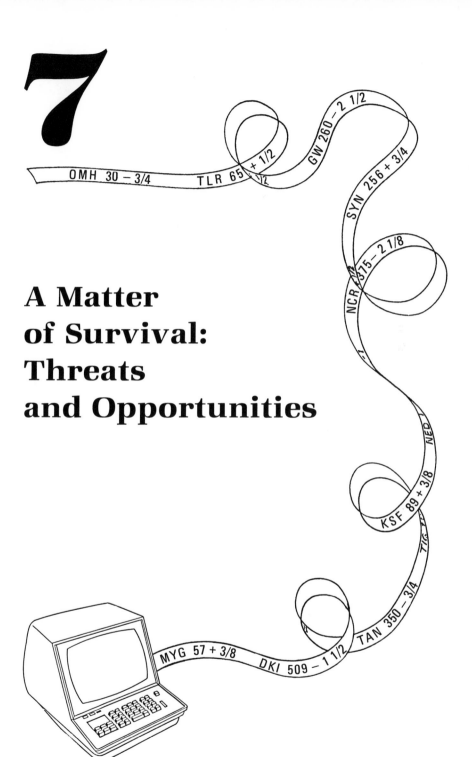

7

A Matter
of Survival:
Threats
and Opportunities

• AN UNEVEN BALANCE

At first blush it seems so unfair. It appears that the financial services revolution is destined to wreak havoc with the many newly created independent producers and the blossoming financial planning movement. The number of threats facing independent advisors and salespeople in the new order far outweigh the opportunities. It is probable that the majority will not survive as Independents, but most will be absorbed into new roles and distribution systems. More than a few forward thinkers, however, will grasp one or more of the available opportunities and enter the new era on a wave of prosperity.

Is the balance truly that uneven? Is it solely the independent producer who will bear the brunt of the storm in the fight for survival? Not really. It may seem that way because the trend reversal will be so dramatic, swinging from rapid expansion to rather pronounced retrenchment. Virtually every group, however, ranging from the consumer through all suppliers and delivery systems, will face serious threats. Each, in turn, will have its offsetting opportunities for those with foresight.

Edward R. Telling, Chairman of the Board of Sears, Roebuck and Company, recently expressed it this way: "The American economic, political and social condition has undergone a radical change—a change that calls out for new products. . .new services. . .new ways of doing business. Old institutions which adapt to these changes will survive and prosper. Those that do not will falter and fail. After all, that is the underlying principle of the free-market system."

Together let's explore some representative groups and see how each will face its own unique threats and opportunities.

- **THE NEW CONSUMER**

If you in the buying public think that you have "got it made" just because you are in control of things after the dust settles—are you in for a surprise! In some ways you could be in as much trouble as those of us who depend on the financial services business for our livelihood. There will be traumatic change. Traumatic change alters lifestyles as well as business customs. Unless you have been reading between the lines as we unfolded the future, you may have missed some of the serious threats facing tomorrow's financial services customers. Now is the time to pay close attention. What you read now may save you a great deal of time and, perhaps, help you avoid the agony of seeing your precious assets misdirected or even wasted.

Think of the many dangers facing the average consumer during and immediately following the financial services revolution. You, the consumer, will be more sophisticated and more knowledgeable of the financial services and products being offered to the public. Smarter, yes—but in many cases, it may be just enough extra knowledge to be dangerous. You'll know enough about the products of tomorrow to feel that you should treat them as commodities. Your job, you will feel, will be to shop for the right supplier and the lowest price.

Although you think you are going for "quality," this tendency to be cheap could result in the purchase of either risky or low quality merchandise. When you are investing your hard-earned dollars, that can be fatal.

The intense new competition, combined with the tendency to stress low cost, may bring about an entirely new generation of poor quality products backed up by either no service or slipshod customer service and record-keeping. More than ever, it will be the old story of "customer beware." You the consumer will have to use your new-found knowledge and access to information via your computer accessed data bases to check and double-check the quality of every purchase you make. While you're at it, you will need to discover new ways to insure that the suitability of your purchase fits, as closely as possible, your financial needs, desires, and risk tolerances.

In addition to the many types of deadbeats that will come crawling out of the discount window when price and price only is overstressed, the entrance of a host of new players into the financial services business may result in some honest but nevertheless equally devastating results. Think about it. Everybody and their uncle will be getting into the financial services act. Particularly at first, this could result in a good deal of confusion. Products and services will be getting more complex, particularly with the simultaneously exploding revolution in electronic linkages. This new complexity, however, will be placed in the hands of fairly naive, inexperienced suppliers. I'm referring to such things as banks selling insurance or, for that matter, the insurance companies offering traditional banking services. You the consumer may occasionally have to pay a price for the learning process of others. Caution will be the order of the day. Be aware, beware and examine each purchase carefully.

Eventually, however, tomorrow's consumer will be the beneficiary of the financial services revolution. The free enterprise system has a way of working those things out, although with so many delivery systems evolving there could be a good bit of confusion at first. Turn back to the chart which spelled out the suppliers and delivery systems of the future. It might be a little confusing for you to decide which delivery system to deal with, let alone what products and services to buy. For the sake of convenience, will you tend to deal with one particular type of delivery system to take care of your financial needs—or will you tend to use them all at one time or another? How will you make that choice? Only you will be able to make that decision, but it will be more in your interest if the decision is made deliberately rather than as a result of advertising thrusts, sales contacts, or even "I did it that way because Uncle Louie did it that way."

In many cases your choices will be somewhat dictated by the marketplace. For example, in the last few years, more and more of you have learned to deal with the so-called independent financial services representative: financial planners, personally producing insurance general agents, and the small independent property and casualty insurance agencies.

They have been enjoyable to do business with because they contact you personally, explain the financial services and products to you face to face, and provide a high degree of service. But, as explained previously, many of those Independents soon will either be not so independent or will be out of business completely. Where does that leave you?

Actually, as fate would have it, it seems that it is going to be the consumer who becomes more independent, not the producer. If you have enjoyed the high level of personalized service that was showered upon you by the independent producers of the past, you will see it diminish. Although still available, service will become crisper, less personal, and more electronic. Many of you are going to have to learn to deal with the not-so-independent "independents" of the future—the Network. Networks have banded together for efficiency and they will deliver a wide variety of products and services. They will not, however, be as personal as the Independents were in the past. You are going to have to do a little digging on your own to get the high quality of service that you have enjoyed in the past. With a little effort on your part, however, Networks will be able to do a very credible and professional job for you.

You'll have many other choices. How about the so-called Captives of the future who will be the full-time, career sales representatives of fully integrated financial services firms? Although a single individual will not be able to be an expert in each and every product line, at least the firms that those salespeople represent will be able to provide you the full spectrum of products and services—theoretically, everything you need at one stopping place! It's starting to get confusing, isn't it? How do you choose among these many distributors of products?

To add to the myriad of choices, you will not be able to avoid seeing the elaborate Financial Centers that will be set up in virtually every major department store in the country. Will you be one of those who do indeed buy their stocks where they buy their socks? It does have a high degree of convenience, although it may not be quite as personal as the service provided you by a Captive or Network professional consulting with you across your desk.

How are you going to be able to resist from time to time sampling the tempting wares of the many Direct Response organizations? The odds are, you won't. More and more operations are going into direct forms of marketing, ranging from the specialty type of products supplier to the many discount organizations that will be forming during the next decade. Very little service, of course, but rock bottom prices! How do you decide? Which products do you buy through this method and which do you buy through a more professional outlet? These will be the decisions facing all of the consumers of the post-revolution age.

Add to all of that the complete privacy, the enormous range of services and the extreme convenience of electronic marketing, and the stage is now set to intensify the confusion that will be rampant in the financial services marketplace. It's not just the suppliers and delivery systems that will be traumatized. You will be right in the middle of it, trying to make your decisions coolly and calmly while the industry pounds at your door trying to get in.

There are other dangers that will face the consumer, particularly during the period when various institutions are attempting to go through the transitions necessitated by the onslaught of the financial services revolution. There will, as stated earlier, be those that do not make it. Most will be merged rather quietly, but some may not be so fortunate. There could be a few outright bankruptcies: banks, insurance companies, perhaps a stockbrokerage or two, and some smaller entities. Should it reach a crisis proportion, some may be bailed out by the federal government. Most likely, however, such firms would meet their demise one by one and you might find yourself the loser. Keep an eye on the organizations you now do business with. Stay up with them: read their annual reports. Given a highly volatile economy, financial crises could develop so frequently that there would be little time for you to adjust. Don't get caught sleeping. Unfortunately, these things could happen and, with a little foresight and research, you can avoid being one of the victims.

One thing is certain. The proliferation of close, personal services provided by the financial services industry is about to reverse itself. There must be increased efficiencies and higher productivity. More product must be supplied at lower costs through each and every sales representative. There will not be much time left for friendly chitchat and close personal relationships. In fact, the advent of Videotex itself foretells the demographic changes to come. Because of electronic linkages, individuals will now be able to move even farther away from population centers, yet still be "at their place of work" electronically at 8:00 A.M. every day. People will live farther apart, further decreasing the chances for close personal relationships. Like it or not, we are becoming an electronic society. Start conditioning your mind to that fact now and it will be easier for you to adjust when it arrives.

• A BUYER'S MARKET

Looking at the bright side, the opportunities available to the consumer of tomorrow from the new financial services business are almost endless. Just look at the choices you will have! Seven general types of distribution systems will be attempting to serve you, and each one of those seven types of systems will have a thousand variations. Indeed it will be a buyer's market! In a way, you will be able to express your own unique personality by choosing to deal with that segment of the financial services business which most closely fits your lifestyle and personality.

With that kind of competition, you will find that with a little diligence you will be able to investigate your purchases and demand real quality. This will be another advantage of the electronic communications explosion: You will be able to check out claims and compare one product with another. You will be in the driver's seat, and, with the exercise of a little caution, you will be able to enjoy a wealth of financial products that previously you may not have had access to.

Like most people, you most likely will be dealing with more than one type of financial services delivery system. You will probably form your own unique personal pattern, using one type of delivery system to purchase one type of product and a totally different type of system for another. Some of you will do 90 percent of your business through one individual and delivery system while others of you will enjoy "shopping" every purchase and covering the waterfront. Again, it will be your personality which will make the selection.

I may sound somewhat like a broken record, but I must say that one of the major opportunities for the consumer of tomorrow is to become computer literate today. I'm not pushing it and I certainly don't sell computers. It's just so obvious—the handwriting has been on the wall for some time now. Don't get left behind. I'm not quite sure how fast it will all develop, but I do know that some type of video technology will change our lives in the 1990s. There will be more services from our homes than we can even imagine now. Just like the telephone and, many years later, the advent of television, home based electronic service is a certainty. It's just a matter of timing. Don't let it leave you behind.

Frankly, although I am exposed to and utilize the world of computers every day in my work, on a personal basis I have avoided learning to operate one! It's kind of funny, actually. I do have a computer terminal right beside my desk at the office and, much to the dismay of all those around me, I seldom even turn it on. The data processing people get very frustrated when I tell them that I chose many years ago not to learn to type and I'm not going to do it now! They really can't understand the contrast: On one hand I am a strong proponent of the use of computers both in business and personal life, yet on the other hand I seem to avoid them like the plague. Although none have suggested yet that I consult a psychologist, I am sure that from time to time it has crossed their minds.

There is one little fact that they don't know, but I will share it with you. I am waiting for the next breakthrough. The technology is already here: All we have to do is link together some existing systems and bring them to the point of being economically feasible. Again, it will happen. The only thing that is in question at this point is the matter of timing. It could be fairly soon.

Imagine yourself somewhere in the not too distant future. Because of recent breakthroughs, you have just added a small room to your home. All you had to do was use up a little attic space and—presto—you have added a media room to your house. It is full of electronic equipment, but, unlike the past, it is not all just stereo equipment. Here is how it works.

It is 6:15 P.M. and you have just come home from work. You heard several times during the day that there was some frantic activity on Wall Street, but you really didn't get the details. You would like to know what happened. Therefore, you walk to the media room and reach out to turn on the computer. It looks much different than the first personal computer you bought back in 1985. It has a rather elaborate visual display and printing device, but there is no keyboard. Just a microphone. After a short warm-up period, you say: "Good evening, Harry. Are you ready to work?"

And the computer answers you: "Good evening. Yes, I am feeling quite fit and all systems are go."

"Then," you say, "I would like to see the New York Stock Exchange closing average, along with the analysis of the degree of change of all the popular indices, and then I would like to see a listing of the most active stocks on the New York Stock Exchange."

"Which data base would you prefer I enter, or should I make the choice?"

"Try Dow Jones, Harry. There may be some subsequent information that I would like to have and it is usually available on their system."

"Right away. I have accessed the data base and the information is coming up now. Here it is."

And then the screen lights up and your data is instantly available.

Yes, that is exactly how it will happen. I will never have to learn to type. I will see the day when I can talk to my own personal computer, it will reply, and it will obey my commands. Yes, there will have to be some training and special programming. But the programs of those days will be extremely "user friendly." The computer will be trained to ask the proper questions to pinpoint your request to give you the desired information. If you think that this is all a little far-fetched, then use your imagination. A healthy mixture of logic and imagination may be necessary for prosperity as we cross over into the 1990s.

Regardless of how it turns out, by all means become computer literate. You don't have to know how to type to learn where computers fit into your professional life and how to utilize them.

There are some other things that you can do to stay one step ahead of the financial services revolution. Do a little homework. Understand the evolution that is going on and the various types of product manufacturers which will exist in the future. Study the distribution systems and see not only how they fit the manufacturer's style, but, more important, how you may use them to your benefit. As you analyze all the systems, don't forget quality. Don't be too tightfisted with the dollar. Be willing to pay for worthwhile services but refuse to pay extra for value not received. Be particular, yes, but reasonable.

There may be other ways that you could benefit from the changes in the financial services world. As enumerated in previous chapters, there will be many new types of mass merchandising. There may be clubs and professional associations you can join that will give you access to products and services that previously weren't even on the horizon. One thing is for sure—there will be many new innovations. Stay alert and try to stay on the leading edge.

Educate yourself. With the proliferation of products, services, manufacturers, and delivery systems, there will be sometimes not-too-subtle pressures to buy almost anything. Electronic marketing, in addition to providing additional financial services, will also bring merchandise of all types into the home. There will be, as in the past, many temptations to spend your money on today's tangibles and ignore tomorrow. Discipline yourself to save and invest. America has one of the lowest rates of saving in the world, placing our population in the hazardous position of being dependent on others (including the government) for their old age sustenance. Force yourself to be responsible and independent.

There are many groups that you could join to assist you in becoming financially independent. For that purpose, a non-profit group known as the National Center for Financial Education was formed just a few years ago. I refer to the NCFE as the fourth phase of the financial planning movement, but in actuality it is totally a consumer's movement and completely divorced from the many financial planning and other professional organizations. In any event, the NCFE has as its sole purpose the education of the public and the encouragement of all consumers to save, invest, and participate in their own financial well-being. Their objectives are worthwhile, and they definitely deserve your support. I would encourage virtually all consumers to become members of the National Center for Financial Education and begin providing for their own financial security today.

Like all of the other players in the financial services revolution, even the consumer group will have its winners and its losers.

• BOARDROOM HYSTERIA

Any established financial services institution which does not today have a certain degree of hysteria in its board meetings just hasn't recognized the problem yet! You think survival is an issue for the Independents? Indeed it is, but not to any greater degree than for some institutions themselves. In a few companies where employment used to be considered taken for granted "until death do you part," employees now are losing their jobs by the thousands. Chief executive officers and chief marketing officers certainly are not exempt from that dilemma. Nothing seems as certain as it used to be—nothing, that is, except constant change. It's enough to create a little hysteria in virtually any boardroom. Definitely ulcer material.

Let's take a look at the threats and opportunities facing the chief marketing officers of organizations which find themselves being thrust into the financial services war. The threats to peace and security are almost endless. First, there are the volatile economic cycles which have begun to plague the financial services business with increasing velocity over the last two decades. There is record-setting inflation followed by periods of relative tranquility. On one hand there are forecasts of lower interest rates, while other gurus on Wall Street tell you that interest rates are about to go through the ceiling. Whatever happens, products, sales patterns, and profits are being affected.

As if an economically driven profit squeeze weren't

bad enough, several other factors simultaneously are putting pressures on the bottom line. Consumers are getting more sophisticated and, hence, more price conscious. They tend to shop more and examine their purchases much more closely before laying out their hard-earned dollars. And then there is the whole tendency toward deregulation, and a rush for more and more manufacturers and distribution systems to get into the financial services arena. The result, of course, of all these factors occurring simultaneously is that there is much less money available for capital investment in the financial services business at a time when there is a demand and need for large capital investments for technology and strengthened distribution systems.

If chief marketing officers haven't gotten the message yet, then they are already in trouble and don't know it. There must be vastly lowered distribution costs. All areas involved in the sales process, ranging from home office and field overhead through the actual commissions paid, must be trimmed. As a result, there must be vast jumps in productivity: more sales made through fewer sales units or salespeople at a much lower unit cost. It can be done and it will be done, but the old guard will resist the changes every step of the way.

The trends above are already upon us and they will intensify in the future. Large, established institutions who for decades have enjoyed the comfort of a relative status quo are now almost desperate to implement constructive change and more effective ways of operating. Many are beginning to realize that they are going to have to trim their bureaucracies and, even more important, change their management styles so that they can henceforth become decisive, responsive, and clear-thinking.

The greatest threat to chief marketing officers in this environment, therefore, is the tendency to hold onto old ways of thinking and operating. The old ways just don't work anymore. Not only must you think differently now, but you must go through the whole process at a much more rapid pace.

If you are a chief marketing officer and you are with

one of those many companies that still is floundering in indecision, I would suggest that you take charge immediately and shake your company firmly by the lapels. Wake them up because there isn't much time left. Some of the decisions are rather obvious if you'll pause occasionally and do some crisp, clear thinking. In fact, that is excellent advice. Occasionally detach yourself from the current demands of the day-to-day business and all of the many types of traditional thinking. Get by yourself and assume that it is your business and you can mold it anyway you want. Write down your ideas. Then go to your chief executive officer and suggest some definite, clear directions.

Aren't some of the decisions becoming rather obvious? If you are a Wholesaler type of supplier, for example, it is possible that you are one of the companies that depend primarily on independent producers for your distribution systems. Pure Independents, however, may become a rapidly dying breed, melding into various types of Networks. Doesn't this tell you that you and your company had better line up your Networks now—or risk losing producers in the future? In fact, perhaps your company could be one of the prime movers in getting Networks together and supplying them with the technology and software that links them to your company. Take the initiative!

It is becoming increasingly clear that the emerging winners in the financial services industry, in fact, will be those supplier organizations which break away from the crowd and refuse to follow the old herd instinct. The market seems to be welcoming small, young companies which have sprung up out of nowhere to provide a special product or serve a particular, specialized market. Even some of the older, more established institutions have shown a degree of aggressiveness, and, when they have, you can see them moving back toward the leadership positions that they used to hold.

There are so many opportunities that you can look for if you will just think a little differently than the crowd thinks. For example, let's assume that your company is now in the Generalist category of suppliers. Your distribution system involves utilizing a captive sales organization made up of professional, career salespeople who, at least in theory, work for you full-time and distribute nothing but your products. You are aware, of course, that in order to lower distribution costs many companies have opted to abandon or circumvent their career field force in order to go after the swelling ranks of Independents. In order to be contemporary, perhaps you are thinking of doing the same thing. Resist the temptation! Explore to see what is really the best thing for your organization. It is quite possible, for example, that at this point you should strengthen your career sales system to get more firmly entrenched in that type of marketing while your competitors are abandoning it. Is it possible that while they are chasing the rainbow of the independent producer you could be working with your career distribution system to make it more efficient? Perhaps you could be molding it into a viable, productive entity. With a little leadership, it is amazing sometimes what a field force will accomplish. You, however, must supply that leadership.

Think of the other things that you could do if you will just break loose from the old lethargy and use your fertile mind. Look for the special situations that tend to create market anomalies. It appears that most Networks and independent producers plan to ignore middle-income America, abandoning that market to the Merchandisers and Discounters. It is possible you could carve out a niche there for your company? There will be many middle-income Americans who still want personalized service. Your challenge will be to accomplish it for them efficiently and economically.

If you are a home office executive another thing that you could do is reread this book carefully, doing a little "reading between the lines." I realize that, like most looks into the future, there are many things in this book that are controversial. Controversial or not, however, if it does nothing more than get you away from your old ways of doing things and into the habit of doing some forward thinking—it will have been well worth the time you spend on it.

Think. Be aggressive. Have the guts to suggest the unusual. Be a mover and a shaker in an industry which historically has been slow to change. Do you think that is a higher personal career risk for you? Frankly, I doubt it. CEO's and CMO's will be the first to go when the bottom line is under pressure. So if you are going to be in danger anyway, why not have fun. Be aggressive and make a contribution. If you really want to be safe, find another line of work. Those days are over.

It's time to face the real world head-on. Recognize the marketplace for what it is. Learn new ways. Here's another rather radical piece of advice to chief marketing officers. Learn to do something that you've never done before: Learn to work in partnership with your company's chief financial officer! For many decades the chief marketing officers of many companies have had the luxury to completely ignore the impact that their many programs and distribution systems may have on profits. Markups in many sections of the financial services industry were so high that tremendously inefficient organizations could still show a handsome profit. You may not enjoy that luxury anymore. You must look at every program with profit and loss in mind. You cannot do it without the assistance of your chief financial officer. Work with him. You will find that you and he may make very good partners during the battles which will ensue in the financial services revolution.

I just cannot resist giving another piece of advice to home office executives of financial services complexes. If you, like so many of us, are from the old school, then get somebody young and sharp on your immediate staff who is computer literate and will stay up-to-date on the progress taking place in electronic marketing. No matter what type of manufacturer or distributor you are, electronic marketing will affect your life and probably do it much sooner than you anticipate. Rather than be surprised, why not be prepared?

• CAPTIVES: DINOSAUR OR DYNAMIC?

"The reports of my death are greatly exaggerated." In 1897 Mark Twain wrote those famous words and sent them in a cable from London to the Associated Press. They would be just as apropos today in addressing the threats and opportunities facing the so-called Captive form of delivery system.

Particularly as the term applies to the life insurance business, industry wags have for the last several years been predicting the complete demise of full-time career distribution systems. Indeed, even I earlier in this book asked the rhetorical question of whether that system was dead. If you remember, I, in effect, said "Yes, as it exists today." I stick by that answer. As it exists today, it is dead. As a system, however, it has every chance of being one of the strongest distribution systems in the financial services business. Let me explain.

The term Captives is a rather broad category applying to all full-time salespeople who work for and distribute the products either manufactured or brokered through one specific manufacturer. Included in the category, therefore, would be all of the stockbrokers in the United States and those insurance people who work for just one company. These range from exclusive life insurance general agents with the large, traditional life insurance companies to the State Farm type agents who distribute various forms of insurance. Most industry professionals started in this category. All told, there are tens of thousands of Captives. In the past, that type of distribution system has been one of the most stable and dependable. It has, however, been one of the most expensive forms of distribution. That made little difference when there were large markups on most financial services products, but the trend toward lower liftoffs and more efficiency has put increasing pressure on the Captive distribution system.

It was reported, for example, that the life insurance industry spent about $250,000 just to train a new life insurance agent and that agent had only a one in five chance way, then they will be free to shop for a better deal from other companies. Their own host company spends thousands in housing and training them, yet on the side they are cheating by going to other companies to get a product with a slightly higher commission. This is not the time to play games. If you are in a Captive distribution system and you are not now loyal, then when the crunch comes you will be the first to be dumped. You're doing things exactly opposite to the way they should be done. This is the time to build loyalties.

Of course another danger that may still be facing some Captive, career salespeople, is that their companies may have been slow to move and are still following the herd. If you are with a relatively small company, for example, which still has a career distribution system, keep an eye on their current pronouncements and activities. If you see that they are blindly going for alternate distribution systems, watch out! They may indeed disband their Captive system and be one of the late entries in trying to go after the Independents. They will lose, but in the meantime you may also. Listen. Understand their attitudes. Protect yourself.

Another threat to the Captive distribution system may also be created by the salespeople themselves. Many salespeople during this revolution are tending to overreact to the company's efforts to try to add profitable new directions. If the company wants to add a new distribution source which is in no way competitive with what you are doing, support it rather than fight it. Be tolerant. Don't simply try to protect your territory and get paid for something you don't do. Keep in mind that unless your company is healthy, you are not going to be better off. Help them through the financial revolution. They, then, will be able to help you.

If you are associated with a Captive distribution system, these are some of the things you can do to create opportunities for yourself. If you are now with a solid firm, stress loyalty rather than rebellion. While others are going astray, this is the time for you to be appreciated.

of surviving in the industry for two years. A quick loo
a few statistics like that when the marketplace
demanding efficiency, and you can see the pressures t
have been developing. Many companies have inc
decided that they can't support a so-called Cap
distribution system and have disbanded theirs. M
other companies have trimmed down their Cap
organizations and, simultaneously, found ways to
cumvent that system in distributing their various fir
cial services products. But what about the remaining (
tive delivery systems? Will they survive in the 1990:

Nothing is safe. Any breaks you get during the r
ten years you'll have to make for yourself! But yes,
believe that the Captive type of distribution system
not only survive but thrive in the 1990s. It will
operate quite differently than it does today and be the
clusive province of the Generalist type of supplier
short, like all other distribution systems, Captives
learn to move more product through fewer salespeopl
a much lower unit cost. Although many salespeopl
those Captive systems are resisting these changes at
time, it will happen and they will adjust. The smart c
may be better off than they were before.

Let's look at some of the threats to the Captives t
they themselves might be able to alleviate if they take
tion now. For example, Captives understand that they
under a great deal of pressure. Instead of learning ho
be more efficient, however, many of them are try
desperately to hang on to old ways. Every time their c
pany makes a change to try to make them more effic
—even ways to help them make more money—they
resist it if it doesn't look like the "old way." They m
learn that fighting the facts won't change the ultim
outcome. All of us—including the Captives—are goin
have to march vigorously into the new world of the 199
or we simply won't survive.

Another threat to the Captive form of distribu
system involves their own current attitudes with reg
to their companies. Many seem to have the feeling th
their own companies won't continue operating in the

Strengthen your relationships. Demonstrate your value. You are going to need an ally during the revolution.

Another opportunity for you right now is to demonstrate your value. Companies are desperately trying to come up with ways to increase productivity. Help them do it. In the process, you will be helping yourself make more money and carve out a future. After all, the Generalists of the future will have many amenities plus products from a whole spectrum of financial services (including products of other companies). Even though you will be a Captive (which means captive to their system), they will make everything available. In many respects, you will look almost like an Independent without the risks. Think it over. Maybe it's not a bad life. Just make sure you're with a strong, forward-thinking company.

If I were a Captive salesperson with a Generalist type of manufacturer, I think I would be busting my garters right now to do everything I could to help my management shape the future. I'd be on my producer councils and offer positive, practical, forward-looking suggestions. I would want to be on the forefront of the revolution, rather than trying to hold on to the old ways which are sure to die. While I was learning to enhance my own productivity, I would also do what I could to help my company become more efficient. Together, in partnership, we could face the future as a unified force.

The threats facing the Captives are mighty and they are many. There are opportunities, however, for those who will make the conscious effort to quit worrying and get to work to build for the future.

• A DECLARATION OF INTERDEPENDENCE

It was in 1983 that Irma Independent finally made the momentous decision. She had agonized about it for slightly over two years and now that she was ready to make the move, she still wasn't 100 percent certain. Irma was a successful professional, so she was doubly cautious about making any move that might endanger her career.

It seemed like so short a time, but actually it was over eleven years ago that she had started in the financial services business as an insurance agent for a large, well-known insurance company. She was what many people refer to as a captive agent because she handled the products of only her parent firm. She did it with her client always uppermost on her mind, however, so she considered herself not a Captive, but a career professional. She did a good job for her clients and, as a result, she had risen to be one of the most respected and highly compensated individuals in her company. Her production qualified her for the prestigious Million Dollar Round Table the second year in the business and she had been a member in good standing of that organization in every subsequent year. She kept up to date and grasped every opportunity to enhance her knowledge. It is a small wonder, therefore, that she was a CLU after just five years in the business and a recognized estate planning professional by the end of her first decade in the insurance business.

About the time she was getting well settled in her professional niche, however, several external factors seemed to be forcing some unexpected and unwanted changes on her methods of operation. First of all, it seemed that her primary product of whole life insurance was coming under increasing pressure and attack. Much of the criticism seemed to be unwarranted, but in light of the unsettled economic times the current product revolution seemed to make a good deal of sense to her. Interest rates were sky-high, yet her traditional product tended to pay a steady but rather low internal rate of return to her customers. A new, seemingly untested product called universal life seemed to be making major inroads. Competition seemed to be intensifying, with new companies springing up around every corner. At a time when her company's primary product seemed to be falling out of vogue, she was feeling new pressures from the home office for blind loyalty and more production. ''Don't be concerned about the customer—just produce blindly," they seemed to be saying. Gradually her earnings began to suffer and Irma started worrying.

1981 was a difficult year in other ways. There seemed to be a new brand of thinking sweeping across the financial services industry and a new breed of professional evolving. Although no one had yet really defined the phrase "financial planning," there nevertheless seemed to be a major financial planning movement afoot throughout the United States. With her earnings suffering as a result of the attacks on her traditional product, Irma started to think about providing other products for her clients. She was bright and could learn how to handle more than her traditional product line and it seemed to make good professional sense for her to fulfill more of the needs of her customers. So Irma petitioned her company to consider offering additional types of products, ranging from the controversial universal life through securities products like mutual funds.

The response was less than warm. The company did agree to sponsor her for the appropriate securities licenses through their small subsidiary broker dealership, but they made every attempt to discourage her from even considering selling anything other than the traditional, old line product. After all, they argued, it had served her well over the last several years and they saw no reason why she should alter her successful pattern. They advised her not to get diverted by the new "flash in the pan" philosophies. It seemed like a continuous campaign to discourage her from her new line of thinking.

Irma fretted and continued to worry. Simultaneously, however, she studied and became knowledgeable in a wider range of financial products. She sat for the appropriate securities exams and passed them with flying colors. She yearned to be able to spread her wings and become not just an insurance professional, but a full-blown financial planning practitioner.

What Irma didn't know was that at the highest levels of the home office of her own company there was a related type of worrying going on. Inflation had taken its toll on her company in more than one way. First, and most obvious, were the soaring costs of nearly all aspects of doing business, ranging from personnel payroll to pens and paper clips. Simultaneously, the insurance industry was learning of the word disintermediation. Billions of dollars were locked into the relatively low yields of traditional ordinary life insurance, yet those policyowners were beginning to realize that they could obtain double-digit interest rates on the newly established money market funds. Literally tens of thousands of policies were either cashed in or loaned to their maximum and the insurance companies experienced a massive outdrain of capital. And if that was not enough, the headquarters officers were now hearing pressures from their salespeople to come out with new types of products which yielded a relatively thin profit margin for the company. They tried to fight the trend. They couldn't ignore the product revolution, however, because smaller companies were springing up for the sole purpose of selling the new types of products. It was easier for the new, smaller companies because they were not saddled with the cost of maintaining existing product lines.

There seemed to be no easy answers for Irma's company, so they started taking a closer look at the cost of maintaining their full-time, career distribution system. Here, like so many companies, they were about to give birth to a strategic error. Instead of leading their existing field force into methods of becoming more efficient, they decided to try it the easy way. They decided that they would put less emphasis on their career distribution system and enter the fray of going after the so-called personally producing independent agent. At first blush, it seemed like that method of distribution would demand a lower level of overhead.

From Irma's point of view, her company's inaction toward her needs and suggestions for an expanded product line were reckless and irresponsible. It had been nearly two years now, and she still saw little response. In fact, it seemed like she was getting less support than she had before. So Irma finally bit the bullet in 1983 and became a pioneer in what turned out to be a large-scale migration of heretofore specialized financial services salespeople into the ranks of independent producers. Irma broke all ties with her company and struck out on her own.

It was difficult at first, much more difficult than Irma had anticipated. Although she had a solid client base, Irma was not accustomed to having to run every detail of her professional life, including the so-called "back office" administrative operations. Additionally, handling a full spectrum of products was administratively much more difficult and involved the complicated regulations of a myriad of state and federal agencies. But Irma was tough and determined, so she overcame the obstacles and gradually established herself in her new environment.

One of the things that made Irma's job easy was the fact that there were literally dozens of companies courting her, showering favors upon her for her attention. Soon she found her office completely outfitted with computer hardware, elaborate software programs, sales literature, and even on-site sales support. She was delighted with all the help and utilized it to the fullest in establishing her prosperous new business.

It didn't take her long to develop a habit, however, of playing one company against the other. There were so many that wanted to deal with her that she didn't mind the risk of irritating one or two. She developed the attitude that she cared only about her profession and her clients and, in effect, the product supplier could play the game her way, or not play the game at all. She treated many of her companies, in fact, rather badly. She made almost unreasonable demands for support as well as high commissions. She rationalized that she needed as much as they would give because she was now carrying her own overhead. Simultaneously, however, she was also demanding the absolute best products from all of her carriers, with the word "best" often meaning the most competitive. It was like a wonderland and she was thoroughly enjoying all the response she was getting: high commissions, low margin products, full support, and even good customer service. She had no ties; she had no loyalties. The companies were Irma's slaves.

Irma flourished in her new professional practice. She had shed the traditional, old ways and had entered the modern world of the independent financial planning practitioner.

Gradually, almost imperceptibly, things began to change. It had been just a few years since Irma had set up her new practice, yet strange new trends seem to be establishing themselves. The consumer, first of all, seemed to be changing in attitude. Personal service seemed to be a little less important than it was before. The average buyers, furthermore, seemed to know a lot more about finances in general and even the products she carried in particular. They seemed to be much more sensitive to pricing and somewhat prone to shopping their financial purchases. Although the consumer focus on product competitiveness seemed to be waning in recent years, suddenly it was raising its ugly head again.

Competition seemed to be springing out of the woodwork from almost every angle. With the emphasis on price and product shopping, the Discounters were making major inroads and actually becoming annoying at times. The banks were claiming to be able to provide financial planning assistance and were wooing their customers into financial purchases in every conceivable way. It didn't seem to be as easy to hold onto a loyal client as it was before.

And then there were those people in Washington, D.C. Couldn't they ever decide on what tax and product legislation they wanted? It seemed like the laws changed every year, often more than once in a year. Just as soon as you got your software programmed to handle taxes in an orderly fashion, they would change the law again. It was hard to keep up with all the reading required to maintain current knowledge, let alone keep the computers programmed.

On top of all that, there seemed to be some sort of technological revolution underway. Irma, of course, had owned a personal computer for years and had even upgraded it several times. She had all types of estate planning and tax planning software, but with all the changes in legislation and regulations it was hard to keep it current. As a small practice, of course, Irma could not afford the many tie-in data bases that were available. But she didn't worry. Somehow she would keep up and stay professionally current.

Then all of a sudden it seemed like most of her product carriers were in some sort of financial problem. Some of the smaller companies having to draw in their horns didn't surprise her, but even some of her major carriers seemed to be acting funny. One of her primary companies merged with another that she was not fond of, and another smaller one dissolved completely. Yet another set up some sort of special distribution system involving some type of national franchise and cancelled her contract entirely. Her other suppliers seemed to be paying less attention to her and there were new negotiations on every new product for lower commissions and less support. Suddenly there were no gifts, no support—no more romancing. The up-to-date software programs that were literally forced upon her previously were no longer available without a big price tag. No one even came to call on her anymore. Irma could not understand what was happening.

In every professional practice there are important turning points, and they will occur even more frequently in the future. Irma felt that she had broken away from the "old ways" and she had. What she didn't realize was that the exhilarating pace of change had once again brought her to a pivotal point. Her new, modern practice had itself suddenly become an "old way."

Irma didn't recognize it as a turning point when one of her primary carriers approached her when they were setting up that strange franchising arrangement. Somehow they were going to form a Network of professionals like herself, with each subscribing to the services provided by the carrier. The individuals would band together their purchasing power and distribution clout, and the company would provide the needed software systems, data bases, and products. It seemed like a pretty good arrangement, but at the time all Irma could think of was that she wanted to maintain her independence. Yes, there was a certain degree of independence in their proposed arrangement, but not total independence. She had fought for that, and she wanted to hold onto it. What she didn't realize then was that her professional practice would wither and die with it.

Irma was caught in the implosion, but she didn't realize until later what had happened. All she could see occurring around her was that suddenly she was without competitive products and prestigious companies anxious to do business with her. Simultaneously, her costs were soaring and her professional support systems were falling into obsolescence. Fast changing regulations, deregulation, legislation. New competitors. Technological revolution. Data bases and Networks that she was excluded from and could not tap into. Suddenly Irma was abandoned, first by her industry, and subsequently by most of her clients.

No, Irma didn't starve to death. She had enjoyed a prosperous decade as a captive salesperson for a fine company and she had enjoyed even greater success during her subsequent decade as an independent financial planning practitioner. She was much too good to give up the ship over a little adversity. Eventually she took a job as chief financial planner for the largest bank in her town and, although she was not quite as affluent as before, she had a steady income. Besides, Irma is strong, shrewd and smart. She will make a comeback someday when she finally realizes what happened during the financial services revolution.

• THREATS — AND MORE THREATS

Intense competition for alternate distribution systems by the many types of product suppliers created a sudden explosion of independent producers. Most of them were enticed from captive types of distribution systems throughout the entire spectrum of the financial services industry: From insurance companies, stockbrokerage firms, and mutual fund houses. New types of distribution companies, third party administrators, specialized product companies and many supporting vendors sprang up almost overnight. The enticements were irresistible: high commissions, elaborate support packages and virtually complete independence.

The categories of independent producers are almost too varied to describe. Many are just an expansion of the types of independent businesses which existed before the explosion, such as insurance "independent agents" who primarily handle property and casualty insurance, and life insurance personally producing general agents. But there are many more of them now and many more categories. Probably the fastest growing segment of the financial services industry is the so-called financial planning movement. A virtually new organization founded in the early 1970s, the International Association of Financial Planners, literally has exploded in membership. Boasting about 25,000 members, the IAFP has created other entities, such as the Institute of Certified Financial Planners. Not all the members of those organizations are independent, but the nucleus is. New Independents are being created every day. Most of them are in clover now. Although they certainly may not be the only category of distribution system which will be adversely impacted by the financial services revolution, the Independents will be the most surprised.

The greatest threat facing the Independent, therefore, is the impending implosion. As new competitive forces enter the marketplace with their own delivery systems, consumers will become even more sensitive to product pricing. Margins will thin and commissions will fall, driving out all but the most efficient and productive Independents.

Another threat facing independent producers is the intensified competition for their particular marketplace. Independents have concentrated on the affluent market and on small business owners for their customer base.

The huge conglomerates, however, are targeting for the identical markets, intensifying competition for the upper-income consumer. There will not be enough of that type of customer to go around.

Although most independent producers have picked up well on the microcomputer advances of the last few years, many of them still may be surprised by the technological revolution which is just around the corner. In fact, the technology is already here. It is its commercial acceptance which will be the revolution. There is no doubt about it: Electronic marketing, transactions, billing, and servicing will leave mom and pop Independents back with the horse and buggy. Most cannot afford the cost of such linkages, let alone the complex data bases which will be necessary to keep up with the industry.

Another danger that most Independents cannot even imagine now is the loss of prime suppliers. The days of picking and choosing product supplier companies will be gone forever. Those suppliers that cannot become Generalists will be turning in increasing numbers to the Discounter and Wholesaler categories. None of them will cater primarily to Independents, but Network distribution could be a strong outlet for Wholesalers. In any event, that leaves the Independents out in the cold. Product sources for Independents will narrow, leaving them to deal primarily with the Wholesalers. The so-called "dealing", however, will be much different than it is today. After the revolution, the Independent will have to deal with the Wholesalers totally on the Wholesalers' terms. That means that the Independent had better have some clout and a strong production base, or he may find his letters and telephone calls unanswered.

New legislation and changing regulations are not of themselves bad, yet they will add a degree of confusion to the industry as they occur in the future with greater frequency. Tax and product legislation, in particular, seems to be up for review more regularly now than at any time in the past. Independent producers without access to responsive research and lobbying clout, therefore, may find themselves in the near future at a severe disadvantage.

The sheer inefficiency of one-on-one selling in an environment requiring high volume and low overhead will strangle many Independents. Although it may not even be conceivable at this point, much higher levels of productivity will have to be achieved in the near future. Institutions and individuals alike will have to become more efficient, placing more product at less cost. Some will be able to do it. Many Independents will not be able to. In my opinion, fee-based financial planning will not have become accepted sufficiently in time to take up the slack. This will be just one more factor, therefore, that will tend to drive the Independent out of the marketplace.

Speaking of markets, keep in mind that the Merchandisers and banks will be making every attempt to capture middle America and the Discounters will be working with associations and employers to wrap up certain occupational groups. If they are successful, and I think that many will be spectacularly so, this will mean a rather sudden loss of markets for many Independents.

Massive, rapid change. All of these factors are moving to reverse the explosion of independent producers and threatening, instead, to drive them back from whence they came. Many will not be able to cope psychologically with this dynamic type of change and shock. Many will choose to ignore the chaos around them, but it will not go away. It is the unaware that will be hurt. Those who have anticipated the revolution, as well as fortifying and preparing themselves, may enjoy bypassing their more naive peers. That alert elite, I fear, may be too few.

• OPPORTUNITIES: FEW BUT GOLDEN

The greatest opportunity that any individual can hope for is a head start. Damon Runyon put it this way: "The race is not always to the swift nor the victory to the strong. . .

but that's the way to bet!" Your greatest opportunity is to start now while we are "between eras." Most will be caught unaware. Assuming you are an independent producer and totally ready and postured for the onslaught, just think of the enormous edge you will have.

One of the secrets to getting a head start, and therefore one of your greatest opportunities, is to target your future markets and modus operandi right now—in advance. So at this moment turn back to the Financial Services 1990s matrix and let your imagination run loose. Imagine operating in the financial services industry in the decade of the 1990s. Search for profit opportunities. Find areas where you could enjoy functioning and could make a valuable contribution. Visualize yourself playing that role to test its viability. Soon you will find a lucrative, satisfying career tailored to your needs and unique talents. Do it now.

If you are an independent producer, keep in mind that pure, unaltered independence will be a very difficult thing to maintain in the 1990s. It would be to your advantage, I would think, to at least keep the subject of networking in the back of your mind as you go through your alternate plans. Think of group power, yet still maintain a large degree of independence. The key word may be interdependence. In any event, map a path. Know where you are going and how you will get there. In the next chapter we will work together and develop those battle plans.

• ADVANCE IMPLEMENTATION

Whether you are looking at the financial services turmoil from the point of view of a consumer, a captive salesperson, a home office employee, or an independent producer, there's no doubt that a little advance implementation will go a long way toward posturing you in the winner's circle. Knowledge is a powerful weapon when used constructively and promptly. You have the opportunity to be in position before most others know they will have to move.

That brings to mind another of Mark Twain's sayings. He once quipped: "When you're being run out of town, get in front and make it look like a parade." Why not get out in front and stay there?

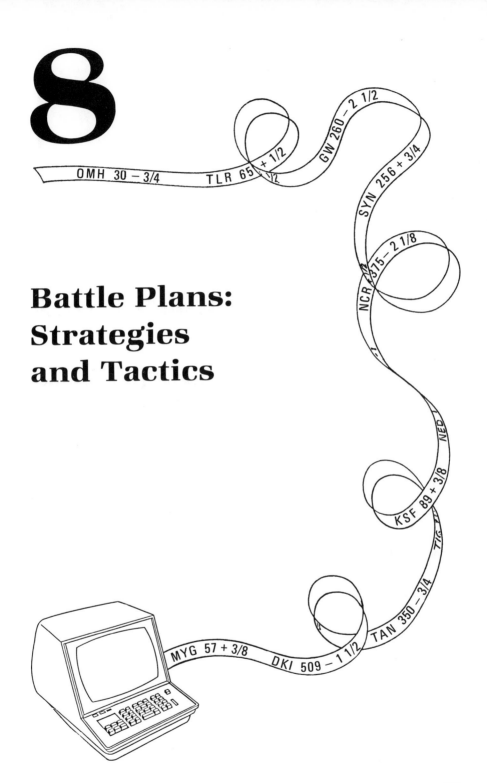

8

Battle Plans:
Strategies
and Tactics

• A MILE IN ANOTHER'S MOCCASINS

The message in this book is aimed at those individuals in the financial services industry who are ready and able to expand their intellectual horizons. It may appeal most strongly to those relatively few who dare to open the curtains in an attempt to visualize the future, but the intended audience includes all aspects and all levels of our industry. Embraced are the suppliers of financial products and services, those who pilot the various distribution systems, and, occasionally, it even talks to each of us in our individual roles as consumers. As you have noticed, however, there is a bias in favor of talking directly to the person who makes the wheels of our industry turn: the professional financial services field representative—the producer—the financial planner—the agent—all individuals who, in one fashion or another, deliver our product to the consumer.

It's not by accident. Although my vantage point now is from the top corporate level, I force myself to try to think like a financial services sales professional. It is not just because many years ago I started my career as a salesman. It's for a much more important reason than that. During the coming revolution, we must all learn to walk at least one mile in the other person's moccasins. No longer can any of us afford to operate in a vacuum. If you are a professional field representative, you had better expand your thinking and understand the pressures I feel as a member of the Board. Similarly, I had better not only have empathy for your position, but also fully understand what motivates you. I must understand what you need to survive the revolution, and what will enable you to ride smoothly through the resulting chaos.

No, we can no longer afford the luxury of operating in a vacuum. You must have a feel for what each segment of the industry is going through now, will go through later and, most important, how each individual segment is likely to react to the new pressures. As you draw your battle plans, keep an eye on how others will react and how the changes in their world will affect yours. As we explore the various possible defensive and offensive tactics, we will attempt to look at each from several perspectives.

• BATTLE PLANS

Stated differently, battle plans is just another way of phrasing the culmination of your own personal planning process. These will be your own individual marching orders which will guide you forcefully into and successfully through the financial services revolution. In a moment, we will explore several possible approaches to the strategic planning process and thereafter we will suggest some specific tactics you may want to use. We will do that just to get your own planning process started—to stimulate your thinking. Only you, of course, can draw your final battle plans, but you had better get about doing it right away. Those who plan to drift aimlessly through the financial services revolution will discover, much too late, that they will not survive.

Now, however, let me give you a word of warning about planning. Keep it simple and, above all, keep it practical! In recent years, particularly at the corporate level, the practice of "strategic planning" has become almost a fetish. Sometimes it is carried to an extreme—to the point where it loses all reason and all practicality. The end result of such planning exercises is that much in precious time and resources are lost. Nothing ever results from such a planning process other than the act of planning itself.

I've seen it happen in more than one company. The intent to do some meaningful one-year and five-year planning was there, but it never really happened in such a form as to positively affect the operation of the company. I can still remember one instance early in my career when I had just been brought out of a field managerial position and given new duties in the home office of a large financial services firm. As fate would have it, our relatively new president had just hired a young business school graduate still wet behind the ears but armed with a sheepskin that proudly displayed his MBA. Given the power of the president's office, this well-intentioned but naive young man ran amuck throughout the company interfering with nearly all operations.

In the name of strategic planning, layers and layers of committees were set up to do nothing but create a multifaceted, drawn-out planning process. Time and time again, department heads were forced to utilize their own personal talents and the resources of their departments to draw elaborate narratives and detailed budgets attempting to forecast expenses (to the nearest cent) for years into the future. It went on for months. Finally, a large separate staff was created just to process all the forms and numbers being created by the formerly productive operating divisions of the company. It seemed everybody was getting totally immersed in the planning process. They were doing planning for planning's sake. It was carried to the extreme, to the point where it was a meaningless exercise.

The end result, at least from a visual point of view, was beautiful. The culmination of the planning process was a whole new library of books and audio-visual materials: notebooks, bound volumes, slide shows, and movies. It was spectacular! And, of course, once it was all produced, everyone in the company heaved a grateful sigh and instantly it was all forgotten. It had been an empty exercise. It became so theoretical that it actually had no relationship to the real world or the real planning process. The only thing that seemed to have been accomplished was the wasting of thousands of work hours that otherwise might have been spent productively. Of course, depending on what position you held with the company, perhaps it was successful in doing one thing: creating dozens of unneeded jobs. The financial services industry can no longer afford this luxury.

Whether your battle plans will be drawn from the corporate level or in terms of the needs of the individual practitioner, don't let the planning exercise get out of hand. Keep it practical. What you need now is a road map to survival and a blueprint for future success. Leave the production of the planning movies to those who erroneously believe that they can still afford them.

• TURNING POINTS

Strategies set forth what you intend to do or accomplish, while tactics detail how you will get it done. We will cover both, but first we must look at strategies. Strategies are paramount because they create critical turning points that could very well affect your entire career.

First you must decide what general direction you will take for the future. Assume, for example, that your present position categorizes you as an Independent in the context of the Financial Services 1990s matrix. That itself is a rather broad category, so let's further boil it down and assume that presently you are an independent financial planner. Now, as you face the impending financial services revolution, you have some choices to make. You do have several alternatives. In light of what you now know, would you be better off in the future as a Captive, as part of a Network, or will you still try to forge your way through as an Independent?

Don't immediately write off the option of being a so-called Captive. That could be a very viable choice for you in the future. As you remember from the matrix, the Captive of the future will be the professional sales representative of the financial services Generalists. That means strength and it also means a certain degree of independence in itself. After all, particularly with the advent of electronic communications devices, financial planners who work for the financial services Generalists in the future will have at their fingertips virtually every category of product available in the financial services industry. That gives you a lot of flexibility as a planner and provides a great many options to your clients. Think about it. Right now, while the so-called Captive systems are somewhat out of favor as they attempt to get their distribution costs under control, it may be an excellent time to establish yourself in that type of distribution system. They will be different in the future, but they will be strong.

Turning points. There are so many of them, particularly as you make career choices. Let's assume that you choose not to go the Captive route as outlined above. You are an independent financial planner and you are dead set on maintaining a certain degree of that independence. You know what the future holds in store, however, so you feel that you may have a problem remaining purely Independent. You realize that you don't have the financial resources to access all of the various electronic marketing outlets and data bases that you will need if you are to represent yourself as a full spectrum financial planner. So you decide that your only choice is to become, somehow, a part of a greater group of individuals who have formed a Network.

Immediately you are faced with yet another decision. What kind of Network will it be? Producer cooperatives will be informal Networks that are stronger than most professional associations, yet preserve the relative independence of the individual as a practitioner. Or should your choice of Network be a franchise, tying you to a national "brand name"? To carry it a step further, professional clusters offer you yet another choice. They are the most formal type of Network, yet individuals in such financial consulting firms do maintain a small degree of independence. If you decide on that option, however, you must then confront many other issues. For example, who will be your partners? How will it be financed? The chain of decisions seems endless.

So suppose you tire of all this and, despite the many warnings which forecast hazards for the pure Independent, you decide to maintain your own financial planning practice. You still have decisions to make then. What will be your method of operation? If you choose personal contact via seminars and interviews, do you have the affluent market to support it? Will you charge fees? Will you have enough distribution power to attract the product suppliers which will be so elusive in the future? If you choose to remain Independent yet wish to utilize electronic marketing, how will you gain access to Videotex facilities? At what market will you aim them?

Regardless of what choices you make, those very choices create need for more decisions and the chain continues to multiply. It is an exercise you must wrestle with, however, until you evolve a crisp, clear set of strategies. Right now you have the option of making your own selections; later they may be thrust upon you, so you might as well face them now. If you wait until tomorrow you may even miss a turning point signal just as Irma Independent did. Force yourself to make those vital decisions now while you can still control your own destiny.

First deal with the strategies and then the tactics. Do not attempt to tackle the latter, however, until you have your strategic directions completed. Only you are capable of drawing up those final battle plans, for only you can know your innermost needs and pinpoint your own unique talents.

Do not read further until your future strategies are crystal clear in your mind. Think them through. Make those decisions. Once that is done, we will then proceed further. Together we will explore the specific tactics you might consider using. Once those tactics are selected, you can combine them with the necessary timetables for accomplishing your objectives. Keep it practical, keep it brief, and then commit it all to writing. Be sure you have a specific deadline for every step. You will then have your own private set of battle plans.

• DEFENSIVE TACTICS

Now that your strategies are completed, it's time to get down to specific tactics. In other words, what methods are you going to use to implement your strategies? How are you going to get there? The choices are endless, but the following selections may stimulate your thinking and start you along the positive path of a definite plan of action. Let's start with defensive tactics.

"Defensive" is the polite way to label it. What I am actually talking about is survival. Not a positive subject, of course, but let's make sure your flanks are protected while you work on your ultimate destiny. No one knows the exact timing, but things will change rapidly. Do not let it sneak up on you. Here are some ideas for fortifying your armor.

Keep in mind the advice to "walk at least a mile in the other person's moccasins." Even though this advice may be aimed at the professional field practitioner, it will be just as valuable to individuals from virtually every discipline in the financial services industry. The implications of the following discussions may or may not be obvious to you, but I can assure you that they will have a profound impact on both your professional and personal life.

• TARGET YOUR PRESENT MARKET

Perhaps the most obvious yet most important defensive tactic is to define your present market, and then, if it fits into your future plans, to start now to carve out a permanent place for yourself within that market. By market, of course, we are referring to the source of your customers. Whether they be individuals or some sort of group association, you must determine what will make you important to them in the future.

As consumers develop more of a price-conscious "commodity" attitude toward products and services, they will tend to become cynical. In the future, they will be more fickle. Up to now, you may have depended upon loyalty to protect your client base. Maybe they simply like you, and maybe they are grateful to you because you have done a good job for them. Don't let that false security lull you into inaction. Those factors will be less important in the future. Loyalty and gratitude may still be factors, of course, but they will no longer be a magnet which draws your clients to you and keeps them within your circle of influence.

Target your present market. Decide exactly what it will be and what it will look like after the financial services revolution. Then determine what it is that the members of that market will need. What can you provide them that is unique to them and that they cannot obtain elsewhere? In the future, the secret of continuing to deal year after year with the same group of clients will be to make them dependent upon you. Not loyalty, not friendliness, not gratitude: You must find a way to make them dependent upon you!

That's a tall order, of course. Perhaps that uniqueness can be found in the type of product or products that you supply to your customers. Or perhaps, via computer technology, you have found a way to unbundle the various products that are available and tie them together again in such a way to provide absolutely tailored financial programs to each client. Perhaps it's product and perhaps it's some unique service. Perhaps it's something that one of your product suppliers provides to you as part of an exclusive list of distributors. Regardless what that unique factor may be in your professional life, it will become your trademark. It will tie your clients to you, because they will become dependent upon it. Start searching for that important ingredient now.

• STRENGTHEN PRESENT RELATIONSHIPS

The relationships I am referring to now are the professional ones, particularly your ties with product suppliers. For the last few years virtually all field representatives in the financial services industry have become somewhat hard to deal with. They are very particular. They want high commissions and the suppliers seem ready to heap those commissions upon them, as well as supplying complete service and elaborate computer systems. There is no end to the horn of plenty—or is there? You had better strengthen your professional relationships with your product suppliers. It is going to be vital in the future to have a primary or host company that will supply most of your products. Give them some reason to hold onto you.

If you are a Captive, for example, you don't have a choice of suppliers, so start now to build a healthy relationship with your host company. You might be well adviced to change your attitude, if necessary, from one of an antagonistic representative demanding higher pay and better products, to one of a partner. Why? Let's look at what are now two fictitious examples, but what in the near future may be an exact picture of what will happen to thousands of individuals.

Charlie Career has been in the financial services business for nearly twenty years, now. He loves it. He has made a good living and he has enjoyed every moment of his relationships with his clients. Charlie just happens to be one of those individuals who is always optimistic. He loves his company and he loves his clients.

In recent years, however, Charlie has felt the pressures of being in a Captive distribution system. Charlie doesn't quite understand it all. He has been with the same company from the very start. His company, in fact, had recruited him from college and sent him to some rather elaborate and expensive training programs. After that, it supplied him with products on which the commissions were ample enough to give Charlie and his family a prestigious place in the community. Furthermore, the company supplied Charlie with a company car, elaborate fringe benefits, and, each and every year, a sales convention at some romantic place in the world. Charlie enjoyed it because he was well off financially and he felt he supplied a worthwhile service for his customers.

The pressures, however, were rising. His company seemed to be cutting back in commissions and fringe benefits. There seemed to be less service, also. Although he never paid much attention to the annual report except when his picture was in it, Charlie did hear that suddenly the company was having trouble making money in certain lines of business. In fact, certain product lines were disbanded. There were even rumors of a search for alternate distribution systems, and fears among many field representatives, that the company would abandon the career system entirely.

Charlie worried, but he was a practical person and he made a decision to continue to be a partner with his company. He understood finances and he knew, in the present environment, that the company must learn to operate with less overhead and that Charlie himself must learn to be a more productive salesperson. So Charlie set out to find a way to accomplish his objectives of making even more money in the face of declining commissions as well as carving a permanent and productive place for himself with his company. Not knowing exactly how to approach his objective, he worked closely with the officials in the sales department of his company. Together, using pilot programs, they developed new techniques and new markets. Rather than one-on-one selling, for example, Charlie learned a new form of semi-mass marketing. He learned certain group selling techniques and became proficient at conducting seminars. He found that he could draw in clients in groups of thirty-five to forty and make a professional presentation which appealed to most of them. Actually, they were eighty percent sold from the seminar. Then Charlie found he could follow up with each individual after the seminar and, in his office and in a relatively short period of time, close his sales in a much more efficient manner than he had in the past.

There were other techniques that Charlie used to make himself a more productive member of the family. An obvious one was to work with his company in actually supplying more products to each customer. His company produced as many of the products as possible, but others that were too expensive to manufacture were brokered in from outside the company. This provided more revenues to Charlie's company and more sources of commissions to Charlie. Everyone seemed to become more productive. The use of the telephone increased in selling and, through upgrading the sales techniques and the clientele, the average financial services order multiplied in size.

Charlie Career was an asset to his company. He became productive and invaluable to them. He was a source of new ideas and a leader in showing others within that distribution system that it was quite possible to multiply productivity in the face of financial pressures.

Clarence Captive was another field representative of the very same company that Charlie worked for. By coincidence, in fact, Charlie and Clarence had started with the company within two weeks of each other. They were pioneers and each was a leading representative of the company. Although they approached their professional duties differently, each had every right to consider himself an outstanding success.

When the financial pressures struck the company, however, Clarence Captive reacted in a much different manner than did his friend, Charlie. Clarence didn't understand it any more than Charlie did, but he felt that all the pressures were negative and each and every one was being forced upon him by the company. Although

Clarence had been a loyal company employee for many years, he began to look upon the home office as an enemy.

At first Clarence resisted any change whatsoever. When the company started losing money on most product lines, the first reaction was to cut costs in the home office as well as in the field. Because of those cost pressures as well as competitive pressures, there was a squeeze on commissions. Faced with making less money for the same volume of sales, Clarence exploded with anger.

The first action that Clarence took was to call several of his associates in the field who were, like Clarence himself, leading producers. Ignoring an existing Field Advisory Board, Clarence convinced his group to form their own association for dealing with the new pressures from the company. Rather than trying to understand what was happening in the financial services business, they decided to resist it. They were not going to tolerate change.

Sessions were set up at the home office between Clarence's group and several highly placed home office executives. The subject of these repeated meetings seemed to center, at first, on commissions and product. The group demanded that the commissions be kept high and, simultaneously, the products kept competitive. In fact, with so many small companies starting up in competition, Clarence's group felt that their own company was falling behind by failing to keep them supplied with "state of the art" products. They demanded that the home office become more efficient. They demanded high commissions, state of the art products, and the most efficient customer services.

In vain, the company tried to explain to Clarence's organized group of salespeople that financial pressures were such that the company could not comply with all of their demands. In fact, they did explain that this captive form of distribution system was expensive to maintain. The company couldn't provide all of these services to their captive distributors and still expect to compete with the upstart companies that provided no services at all and, in fact, supported no distribution system. Clarence could have cared less and he made his feelings clear.

In time Clarence seemed to have a majority of the field distribution system organized in opposition to virtually everything the company was trying to accomplish. In reaction, the company searched for alternate distribution systems that would allow them to distribute their products more efficiently. Some executives in the home office even hoped that an alternate distribution system could be found which would be large enough to allow them to abandon the Captive distribution system entirely. With diligent work, and despite objections from the field, the company was able to establish an alternate distribution system utilizing direct response techniques. It was successful and it was profitable.

It didn't take long for Clarence's group to find out that the company had established a successful alternate distribution system. Still, it was a fact that over 70 percent of the new business came from the traditional, Captive distribution system. The company did not want to jeopardize that position, so it continued to meet with and try to placate Clarence's group. Finding out about the direct response program, however, the immediate response from Clarence's associates was to demand an override on everything that was produced from that new distribution system. They made no contribution to the distribution of products through direct response, but they did want to get paid for it. The company tried to respond, but they found that when they paid an override to those who made no contribution they were back in the old traditional methods of high cost forms of distribution. Despite the fact that they were receiving overrides, Clarence's group did everything they could to try to damage the new program. They talked to individuals in the home office to try to discourage them from supporting the new program and, whenever possible, they told prospective customers it was not a worthwhile product to buy. In effect, Clarence's group began working against its own company. Somehow they failed to realize that by damaging the financial integrity of their own firm, they were sealing their own fate. They could not see beyond today.

Clarence was so active in demanding the maintenance of the old ways, as well as insisting on sharing the fruits of new distribution systems, that his own productivity declined. His timing couldn't have been worse. Things seemed to be changing even more rapidly, now. The company seemed to have developed, out of necessity, an "up or out" type of program to increase productivity. Those who continued to demand high commissions and competitive products, while failing to increase productivity, suddenly found themselves unemployed. It wasn't a vindictive action: the company just did it to survive. They had to raise productivity. The company was fortunate in that it had a core of field representatives, like Charlie Career, who were indeed responding to the need to provide the public more product at a lower cost. The people like Charlie, along with the company, would survive after the new drastic actions were taken—unfortunately, Clarence would not. Because of the elimination of people like Clarence, the actual size of the distribution system shrank. The remaining individuals, however, learned the new ways of the financial services world. Many prospered and the revamped Captive distribution system, at last running efficiently, flourished.

Stories like the above will be commonplace before long. Strengthen your present relationships with your product suppliers. It is going to be important to have a primary or host company whether you are an Independent, a Network, or a Captive. The programs to enhance productivity will result in "up or out" choices throughout the industry. Prepare yourself and be in the favored group.

• **STAY INFORMED**

Another defensive tactic which may seem obvious but which cannot be underestimated is simply to stay informed. Don't be naive or be lulled into the status quo just because there may be a calm before the storm. You must continue to anticipate rapid change, because it is going on all around you at this very moment whether you see it or not. Continue to keep a flexible attitude, and, even when your battle plans are drawn, have some contingency plans. Watch for avenues of opportunity which may open suddenly and close just as precipitously. Stay active in your professional association and be close to any sub-groups or committees within that association that ad-dress themselves to the many changes going on in the financial services industry. Read like you have never read before, but not just professional publications. Read and understand what the consumer is now thinking and do-ing. Watch the advances in electronic linkages. Keep an eye on the many partnerships that are being formed to develop Networks and Videotex outlets. Stay in touch with home office executives who have the experience and imagination to recognize changes before and during their occurrence. Mental alterness and agility were never more important than they will be during the revolution.

As part of staying informed, be sure that you con-tinue to understand the various cross-currents going on in the financial services business. Listen to what people in your profession are saying. You can't protect yourself or progress in your career by remaining in your own self-centered shell. There are too many outside forces beyond your control. Learn the problems and pressures facing others in your industry and you will have more ammuni-tion with which to insure your own progress.

● **STRIVE FOR EFFICIENCY**

The message here is short and clear. It has been repeated many times, in one way or another, in the preceding chapters. A mandatory survival tactic will be to enhance your own productivity. Do it now. Make the adjustment now while there is still time to do it and time to do it gradually. Spend your creative energies in determining how you can get it accomplished. Like Charlie Career, you may have to work it out by trial and error, but you must do it now. When the demand for greatly enhanced productivity culminates, things will come together fast. If you wait until then, you may not have time to adjust. Do it now. No one is sure when that deadline will be upon you.

• BE TECHNICALLY COMPETENT

Being technically competent can take in a broad range of subjects ranging from knowing the intricacies of your own business to being thoroughly proficient in the use of computer technology. In this context, I am referring to as much of that spectrum as possible. You must be technically competent in your own profession and, generally, computer literate. I'm not saying that you have to be a computer whiz. You must, however, keep up with the latest developments, new technology, and innovative applications. You must understand when and where computer networking is being used and you must have the wisdom to apply it to your own portion of the financial services business.

Whether your duties and career lie in the home office environment or in a distribution system, force yourself and your organization to invest in both equipment and education. Some still try to hang on for dear life, but the old ways are dead. Learn the new ways and participate in the new financial services world.

• KEEP YOUR TRAIN ON THE PRESENT TRACK

Just because things are going to change is no reason for you to make imprudent decisions. Keep your train on the present track until you decide where and when you will switch to your new main line. Until that time, do stay on the present track, but learn to do it more efficiently.

If your responsibilities include decision making at the home office level, get outside research and ideas. Such information must be screened carefully to make sure it results in practical action recommendations, but such outside thinking is needed in our industry. The financial services industry tends to be too inbred, resulting in a lack of new ideas circulating around the system. Some outside fresh air would be welcome, but it must be tempered with experience and mature business judgment.

Before long, a good bit of outside thinking will be forced upon the industry just by the new players that are coming on stream. The banks are not contributing much original thinking at this time, but they will. The new distribution groups that will form also will be sources of new ideas. All the more reason, of course, to keep your ear to the ground.

While you are at it, it will make sense to keep your finger on the pulse of the consumer. Whether you are in the home office or in the field, occasionally survey your own customers, especially the newer ones. Use focus groups. Listen to their ideas. Appreciate what they are telling you. If you don't listen now and make preparations, you may feel the weight of the entire financial services revolution falling upon your shoulders in a very short time. Without advance preparation, it could be too much weight for you to handle at that time.

By all means, keep working on your battle plans. That is the ultimate defensive tactic. Keep working on them until they make sense and offer you a clear path. Map contingencies. Keep fine tuning them. Decide where you will be heading and what your final destination will be.

• OFFENSIVE TACTICS

Spelled another way, offensive, in this context, means prosperity. The defensive tactics are vital because they spell survival, but the offensive tactics are more fun because they build the bridge to your personal rainbow. As usual, there are probably thousands of paths that you can explore and develop. With continued diligence and a great deal of careful thought, eventually they will filter down to the specific map that will not only lead you through the labyrinth of the revolution, but posture you in a leadership position after the dust settles. Here are some ideas you may want to consider.

• INNOVATION

Gypsy Rose Lee reportedly stated it this way: "You've got to have a gimmick!" There is nothing more valuable than good, old-fashioned Yankee ingenuity.

There is more than one way to get involved in innovative ideas and programs. First of all, you should continuously remind yourself and force yourself to expand your thinking beyond your present situation. Use your imagination to think of new ways of doing things. Continuously be positive and be a contributor, but always question the status quo and try to devise better ways.

It's always good advice to attempt to associate yourself with men and women of vision. Although they may be rare, you can find such people involved in all aspects of the financial services business. Many of them are positive, hard-working producers who are now successful and will continue to be successful because they are staying one step ahead of the competition. They are the people thinking positively, not the ones spreading gloom and doom while offering no suggestions for a cure.

At the executive level, too, many individuals are coming out of their old, traditional shells to address the new challenges. Find those people and associate yourself with them. They are relatively easy to spot. In addition to having fresh ideas, these are the people who are putting together programs to try to prove their concepts. During the next few years there will be many pilot programs conducted by the wise companies, because no one has all of the answers at this time. It makes sense for a company to try something on a limited basis to see if it works, and then evaluate it. If a pilot doesn't meet expectations, have the fortitude to admit the failure and stop the program. If it is successful, then have the wisdom to reinforce the program and expand it. My advice to you, whether you are a producer or a home office executive is this: Get involved in these pilot programs. You will learn from them, and, from those that are successful, you will be armed with many valuable innovations for the post-revolution era.

While we are on the subject of innovation, let me make one additional suggestion. It is time that all financial services institutions start encouraging such innovation, rather than continuing to foster traditional, bureaucratic behavior. Those executives who are in control of those institutions would do well to listen carefully to the recommendations that are being made. A lot of talk goes on at the higher levels, but in the past very little innovative thinking was tolerated. Now it should be encouraged, recognized, and rewarded. That will be a radical change at some stodgy old companies, but that is the price of survival.

• RESULTS: THE ONLY RELIABLE YARDSTICK

There was a day—the good old days—when the financial services institutions could measure individuals on the basis of their personality. Whether an executive or a field representative, the key to success was getting along with other people and being the type of person that people like a lot. Heaven forbid it ever be admitted, but it was a fact that in the hallowed halls of many of our greatest institutions, the art of politics was the only profession practiced. All that is just one more set of luxuries that we can no longer afford.

It is time for results. Ready or not, we all must begin to measure everything by what is accomplished. Activity counts for nothing. Politics count for nothing. Long meetings and fluid conversation count for nothing. Complaining and criticism—unless it is constructive—is for naught. Accomplishments—measurable, profitable results—are all that count.

Similarly, it is time for straight talk. "Blowing smoke" no longer has any lasting effect. Regardless of your responsibilities, you must learn to cast your lot with those who know what is happening and are willing to take positive action. It is vital, for example, that supplier companies communicate fully with their various distribution systems. In addition to letting them know that you care, it is time to keep them informed. If they are not educated, they cannot assist you in making the necessary transformations which will allow survival and prosperity in the financial services revolution. Keep your sales force informed and tell them the truth. While you are at it, why not lay all of the cards on the table and ask them for their advice? That not only gets them involved and interested, but you may be surprised to find out that through such tactics you may discover the appropriate answers to your problems.

It is rather interesting to watch some of the things that are going on as the pressures of the financial services business start to build. Many companies are looking for alternate distribution systems. That is a fact and the whole industry knows it. Chasing those available dollars are some legitimate schemes and, unfortunately, many that are ill-conceived. The financial services business is unsettled, leaving the door open for "big deals"—the lure of fast successes, the easy way. There is no easy way. There is no easy "big deal." You know it and I know it. Yet in striving to show some progress many institutions have lost millions in poorly researched, impractical schemes that never had the slightest chance of success.

Yes, it is time for results. We must have results and can only measure progress in terms of results. To prevent imprudent actions, however, we must make sure that we have full disclosure from all parties. Insist on straight talk; insist on results. Trust only those that will operate by those rules. None of us can afford many more false starts.

• **ANALYZE YOUR PRESENT CLIENTELE**

With so much happening, sometimes we may have a tendancy to overlook the obvious. Don't ever forget your present clientele. In light of the changes to come, you may have acres of diamonds right in your own back yard. For example, do you deal primarily with a mature market—that is, with individuals over the age of fifty? It is likely that many of them will revolt against the "dehumanizing" new electronic marketing methods. They will want personalized, face-to-face service. If they are an affluent clientele, that spells relatively big orders, but lower volume. For cost efficiency, therefore, you may find that under such circumstances you need to charge fees for your services. Keep in mind that this also is a time for tough, factual thinking. If in such a situation your market cannot support fees, find a new market. You would be no good to them from the poorhouse.

While individual distributors are deciding what distribution system they will occupy in the future, it is, simultaneously, time for the head offices of financial services institutions to do similar soul searching. It is time to be shrewd in choosing future courses, and aggressive in implementing new strategies. The key is making rational decisions before the time comes when those decisions are forced upon you within a very short time frame. For example, each and every institution must decide what type of product and service supplier they will be. In which of the five categories will they ultimately reside? Once the supplier category is determined, then there is the choice of delivery systems. Although influenced to a great extent by the supplier category, the delivery system selected must be compatible with the firm's operational style and the client base that the firm plans to serve.

If you are an independent producer, be aware that those types of decisions are taking place in the executive offices of every one of your suppliers. Like it or not, in the near future you may have to sacrifice a good bit of your independence. No, I'm not saying that the role of the Independent will completely disappear or that the burgeoning financial planning movement is dead. It is just that they and you will not be as purely independent in the future as you would like. If you let it surprise you, you may not be in business at all. If you prepare for it, then you will be able to make the necessary adjustment to operate in the new environment. In fact, it is not the changes as such that will eliminate so many small operations. The cause actually will be the fact that they didn't know the changes were coming and they did not prepare.

• UNPLUG THE DECISION-MAKING PROCESS

Whether you are an individual producer trying to form some sort of Network or an executive trying to posture your firm for success, one thing is certain. The decision-making process must be faster. No longer will situations be tolerated where months and sometimes years go by before any action is taken on a positive suggestion.

For individuals, this means that the responsible practitioner will have to force decisions. For example, if you are trying to do a joint project through your professional association, you will find that decisions seldom will be made as long as no one is fully responsible. Take the bull by the horns. You become the responsible party. Bring the issues at hand to the forefront, make them visible to everyone and form a consensus. Don't let important decisions float on unresolved. There is not enough time left for that.

For institutions, the job of unplugging the decision making process will not be that easy. Forward-looking executives at the highest levels are going to have to find some way to unwind the massive bureaucracies which stand in the way of swift, intelligent decision making. A good place to start would be an examination of the entire committee system. Committees take up an enormous amount of people's time and unless such committees have a specific purpose, they should be disbanded. To make sure that sufficient communication still flows within head offices, in the place of committees there could be periodic meetings of department heads and managers at various levels to foster communication on the status of current projects.

Another way I found to encourage decision making within large institutions is the formation of project teams for specific purposes. Charge them with an objective, give them a deadline, delegate enough responsibility and authority and often you will find that a project is completed quickly and all problems have been solved without the involvement of higher management. There is a lot to be said for a matrix management type of task force system, because the minds of individuals at all levels can be productive. The secret to successful project teams is having a good leader and involving one team member from every involved department in the company. As long as the proper amount of authority is delegated to each individual team member, the job can be done swiftly and efficiently. When the project is completed, the project team actually dissolves so that a perpetual committee is not formed. It had one task, it completed that task, and then it dissolved.

There are many other techniques for enhancing the decision-making process, and the details have been explored in several management books. Suffice it to say here, however, that decision making must be a more rapid process in the financial services industry. We must unplug the system now, because the need for decisions will come rapidly once the full fury of the financial services hurricane starts to unleash itself.

• PURSUE ELECTRONIC MARKETING

Get involved in Videotex and the whole world of electronic marketing—now! Contact research groups, cable TV companies, telephone companies, and even your local television stations. Find out what is going on in that field in your locality. They will need pioneers to test the new methods. If you have the opportunity, why not make it your hobby? Donating a little time today will pay big dividends tomorrow. I hate to date myself, but I can remember the pioneers of a new communications vehicle called television many years ago. Tiny screens and almost obscure, scratchy pictures. We laughed. So did the pioneers—all the way to the bank.

Check around. You may be surprised to discover that your own company or product supplier has a research department that somehow is connected to one of the new Videotex experiments. Again, volunteer to participate in any way you can. This is the time to learn and this is the time to get a ground floor position. Maybe it won't have a great influence on your future career, but it will have a profound influence on our industry in general. That alone is reason enough for you to stay close enough to it that you will be able to make a "go/no go" decision sometime in the future. You can join it or not, depending on circumstances at that time. But by being involved now, you will know enough to keep it from burying you.

- **IDENTIFY PRIME PRODUCT AND SERVICE SUPPLIERS**

I can't say it too often. Although they may be chasing you now, the suppliers of the future will be finicky and hard to please. If you are one of those many financial services salespeople who are using the present cycle to choose only the loss leaders from each company to sell, enjoy your picnic. The only problem is the fact that the picnic will soon be over and you may be left with only the crumbs. Frankly, I can't blame you much for taking advantage of the current situation. The naive companies are doing almost everything they can to lure the many newly created independent producers, and the resulting competition is causing many to offer products that are subsidized and actually create losses on the income statement. The thinking is that they will use these loss leaders to attract the loyalty of the many producers out there and that the profits will be made later when those producers sell the full spectrum of the product line of the supplier. That's not the way it's working, however. The companies are losing their shirts—and it is hard to make that up in volume! The end result is rather obvious to anyone who wants to look into it, yet most of us continue merrily on our way hoping that somehow everything will correct itself. It will, but only because the suppliers suddenly will get tough. They will become picky and less cooperative in the future, seeking to eliminate forever the unprofitable type of producer that they have attracted to their ranks.

This is the time, therefore, to identify your prime suppliers and try to build some permanent relationship with them. In fact, while they are still eager to accommodate, why not try to lock some of them in as much as possible with long-term contractual agreements? Line up the ones you deal with and give them as much business now as possible. Don't shotgun your production. Let one company or a small group of companies know that they are your favorites and that they can depend on you.

Do not totally box yourself in, however, because you have no way to know whether or not you are dealing with a survivor when you pick a supplier. Have backups selected and ready. Go with your favorite, but watch their income statement and balance sheet. Watch their business decisions. Make sure that you are in partnership with a survivor company.

Just for a minute, let's look at this whole thing from a consumer's point of view. After all, each of us is a consumer. If it is true that there is to be an implosion among the ranks of totally independent financial planners and other financial services producers, doesn't it make sense to develop some lasting relationships right now? Pick somebody competent, yet make sure it is someone strong enough to survive the coming financial strains. Develop a strong relationship with a financial services representative that you respect and trust. Although right now you may need them more than they need you, the roles will be reversed in the not too distant future. They will need you and need you badly. As a consumer, take advantage of that, and, as a consumer, select a topnotch professional as your financial advisor today.

• FEE-BASED PRACTICES

If you plan to charge fees, proceed with caution and careful thought. First of all, totally fee-based practices have caught on very slowly and only with a very limited clientele. It is talked about a lot, but not practiced as much as many would like you to think. Now add to that the influences that the future will bring. The Discounters will make major penetrations via direct mail and Videotex. The Merchandisers will be tempting your customers with prominently displayed financial merchandise in every department store. If you are going to attempt to charge fees, you better have lined up a prestigious clientele and established a justification for those fees. It won't be easy.

Again, a little imaginative thinking is in order if you feel that your future involves establishing a fee-based financial planning practice. First of all, as in all other aspects of the financial services revolution, you must have alternatives and contingencies. Once those are established, you can come up with some innovative ideas for making your fee practice prosperous while others may not be so fortunate. As just one idea, perhaps you can combine your fee practice with the distribution of no-load products to beat the Discounters at their own game.

• NETWORKS: YOUR SAFETY NET?

Frankly, I feel that some sort of networking procedure will be absolutely mandatory for any producer—whether Independent or Captive—for survival both during and after the financial services revolution. It will be impossible to operate in a vacuum. Either you join together formally with a group of individuals for buying power and information networking, or you will find yourself becoming totally obsolete.

You must, therefore, start now in establishing your Network. Most professional associations provide little more than a magazine, a few meetings, and maybe a convention, so they will be of little help. Should you take the initiative to start a producers cooperative or do you feel you can receive the necessary linkages through a vendor, product supplier or NASD dealer? If you decide on one of the later choices, once again you had better have a backup or two ready in the wings. The vendor, supplier or dealer that you choose may not be in business in the 1990s and I can assure you that you will not be operational without direct electronic linkages for communications, research, market access, instant transactions, billing, and customer service. If you are an independent producer, then believe this. You can take this advice to the bank. You will need these things. You must decide on some sort of networking procedure to preserve at least some degree of your own independence. Now is the time to start the wheels in motion.

Don't overlook the most sophisticated form of Network. You may want to investigate the possibility of joining a few other specialists in the formation of a professional cluster. Professional clusters will be a major market force in the 1990s. Some practitioners will make millions with this tactic alone.

Although categorized separately, the Captives will have all of the advantages of a Network. Their Generalist host companies will provide the necessary services, electronic linkages, and product diversity. The more formal structures and generally larger sizes of Captive distribution systems may provide extra strength in coping with the shifting sands of constant change. Don't ignore them as a viable choice. It was no accident that Captives was one of only four types of primary distribution systems which survived on the Financial Services 1990s matrix.

One of them might very well provide you a comfortable and profitable professional operating base in the future.

• TRACK THE BOOMERS

This tactic is not optional. Keep close track of what the baby boomers are thinking and doing. The baby-boomer market is an emerging one and one that will have considerable impact on all markets in the future. Whether you deal with them or not, they will alter your habits and the habits of the individuals who constitute your distribution market. So watch the boomers. See what they are doing, buying, and thinking. Keep in mind that they are comfortable with modern electronic technology and either own now or plan to soon purchase the hardware. They are a formidable market and one which can be reached electronically. Whether you like it or not, you will be affected by them. Rather than let them control you, maybe you yourself should be involved. In the financial services revolution, those who do not control the circumstances around them will be controlled by them.

These have been just a few tactics to get your creative juices flowing and to start the thinking process. Now that you have started down the road, keep moving. Keep thinking. Make notes. Narrow your choices to those that fit your personality, talents, and market. Formalize your battle plans. Enter the financial services revolution with your eyes open and your head held high. Know where you are going and be determined to reach your objective.

• TODAY

The powerful forces at work to revolutionize our industry still remain submerged but they are making headway at a breathtaking pace. Which waves will crest first no one knows. Only that they will show themselves soon is certain.

Fasten your life preserver, tighten your seat belt, and batten down the hatches. Then start rowing like hell. Steer your ship, first, to flow with the turbulence, and, ultimately, to navigate to your personal port in the storm.

Plot that course today. Your trip may begin sooner than you think.